The Perishable Empire

The Perishable Empire
Essays on Indian Writing in English

Meenakshi Mukherjee

OXFORD
UNIVERSITY PRESS

OXFORD

UNIVERSITY PRESS

YMCA Library Building, Jai Singh Road, New Delhi 110 001

Oxford University Press is a department of the University of Oxford. It furthers the
University's objective of excellence in research, scholarship, and education
by publishing worldwide in

Oxford   New York

Auckland   Bangkok   Buenos Aires   Cape Town   Chennai
Dar es Salaam   Delhi   Hong Kong   Istanbul   Karachi   Kolkata
Kuala Lumpur   Madrid   Melbourne   Mexico City   Mumbai   Nairobi
São Paulo   Shanghai   Singapore   Taipei   Tokyo   Toronto

with an associated company in Berlin

Oxford is a registered trade mark of Oxford University Press
in the UK and in certain other countries

Published in India
By Oxford University Press, New Delhi

ISBN 019 565147 2

Printed in India by Saurabh Print-O-Pack, NOIDA, U.P.
Published by Manzar Khan, Oxford University Press
YMCA Library Building, Jai Singh Road, New Delhi 110 001

To my daughters Rukmini and Rohini
who have gone beyond my textual concern with
India to engage with actual ground-level issues

Contents

The sceptre may pass away from us. Unforeseen accidents may derange our most profound schemes of policy. Victory may be inconstant to our arms. But there are triumphs which are followed by no reverse. There is an empire exempt from all natural causes of decay. Those triumphs are the pacific triumphs of reason over barbarism; that empire is the imperishable empire of our arts and our morals, our literature and our laws.

— Thomas Babington Macaulay
Speech on the Government of India, 1833

Preface

When Thomas Babington Macaulay spoke of 'the imperishable empire of our arts ... and literature ...' which would outlast the sceptre, he could not have anticipated the way history would rewrite the terms of this continuity. The present volume is an attempt to consider the complex and evolving relationship between English and India through literary texts that emerged out of this contact from the mid-nineteenth century to the end of the millennium. I have tried to take into consideration in this study the layered context of the other Indian languages surrounding English, and the intricate socio-economic pressures that impinge on literary production.

The essays are arranged chronologically, the first section dealing mostly with the nineteenth century and the second with the present. Except for four essays which are new, and written specifically for this volume, the other essays, or their earlier versions, have been published in different places within the last decade. But a continuity of concern runs through them. I am grateful to my friend Rajeshwari Sunder Rajan who first pointed this out to me and insisted that I bring them together. My thanks are also due to many others, too many to list here, who have helped me with my work at various stages — by getting rare documents photocopied, by sharing books and information, contributing ideas and commenting on earlier drafts. I specially mention Shubhendu Mund who has most generously shared with me all his research on nineteenth-century Indian writing in English even before his own book on the subject came out; Priya Joshi who made available to me a lot of material from her own archival work; Rebecca Douglas who sent me photocopies of crucial parts of old novels and offered to do more, an offer I failed to take up; Supriya and Sukanta Chaudhuri whose invitation to visit the English Department at Jadavpur University enabled me to spend a month reading old books in the National Library; G.J.V. Prasad who acted as the sounding board for many of my ideas and helped me to untangle certain knots; and Harish Trivedi arguing with whom on different issues has helped me more than he knows. Finally, to Sujit Mukherjee for support as well as criticism and for his timely reminder that completing a book is more important than attending conferences.

The essay 'The First Indian English Novel' has been reworked from the Foreword and Afterword I wrote for the reprint of *Rajmohan's Wife* (New Delhi: Ravi Dayal Publisher, 1996). 'Defective Acoustics in Colonial India' was presented at a conference at Birkbeck College, London, and has appeared in *Women's Poetry, Late Romantic to Late Victorian: Gender and Genre, 1830–1900* edited by Isobel Armstrong and Virginia Blain (London, Macmillan Press, 1999). 'We Say Desh: The Other Nirad Babu' combines two essays, one published in *Nirad Chaudhuri: The First Hundred Years* edited by Swapan Dasgupta (Delhi: Harper Collins, 1997) and the other presented at a University of Hyderabad conference on 'Nirad 100; India 50' in 1998. 'Maps and Mirrors' was included in the CULT edition of *The Shadow Lines* by Amitav Ghosh (Delhi: Oxford University Press, 1995). Two different versions of the essay on *Haroun and the Sea of Stories* were published in *The Postmodern Indian English Novel* edited by Viney Kirpal (Delhi: Allied Publishers, 1996) and in *Ariel* (vol. 29, no. 1, January 1998). 'The Anxiety of Indianness' was published in *Economic and Political Weekly*, November 1993.

Some of the essays published for the first time in this volume have been presented in their earlier avatars in different conferences and seminars — in the University of California at Berkeley; at Montreal (a conference on Postcolonial Translation organized jointly by the University of Concordia and the University of Montreal); at University of Canberra, Delhi University, Asiatic Society (Mumbai), Dhvanyaloka (Mysore) and Osmania University (Hyderabad). I have benefited from the discussions that followed and acknowledge my debt to those who offered comments and raised questions.

Hyderabad   MEENAKSHI MUKHERJEE
3rd March 2000

1

Nation, Novel, Language

When the Prince of Wales visited India in 1875, amidst the variety of responses generated by the event — ranging from the celebratory to the critical — a satirical piece appeared in *Bangadarshan*, a Bangla periodical. Written as a fictitious dispatch by one of the special correspondents who was supposed to have accompanied the Prince to India, the article contained the following passage:

From Sir William Jones upto Max Mueller, many Orientalist scholars tell us that there is a language in India called Sanskrit. But after coming here I have not heard a single person speak that language, nor seen anyone write it. Therefore I do not believe in the existence of this language. The whole thing is likely to be a trick played on us by Messers Jones and the rest who have invented this language to acquire respectability for themselves.[1]

There is an asterisk in the text at this point, followed by a footnote which warns the reader not to consider this funny: 'Caution. No one should laugh at this. The great scholar Dugald Stuart actually holds this view.'

I use this quotation to underscore the refiguration in the hierarchy of languages taking place in the wake of the Orientalist/Anglicist debate on education that raged in India during the early decades of the nineteenth century, culminating in the much-discussed Minute on Indian Education in 1835. Within half a century the ground of discourse had shifted; one of the main contenders of power, Sanskrit, had not only ceased to stake its claim in the sphere of knowledge and power, but was being defended by the Bangla press — although ironically — to remind the rulers of its existence. The Orientalist lobby having virtually conceded defeat, the transaction was now between Bangla and English in and around Calcutta, as it was between Marathi and English in and around Bombay as far as knowledge and cultural production were concerned, with the local language assuming centrality in creative literature. In one of his six major essays on Bengal — pertaining to its history, culture and language — Bankimchandra Chatterjee (1838–94) argued in the last quarter of the nineteenth century that the Bangla language itself had become a site for contestation between Sanskrit and English, one pulling it towards a heavily stylized diction and syntax — sonorous and formal — while the model of English deflected its growth towards a relatively informal prose, closer to the language actually spoken by the upper classes in the urban areas.[2] He mocked the last-ditch attempt made by the Sanskrit pandits, unsure of their own position, to control Bangla, which was emerging as the dominant language of literature in the eastern region.

In 1835, when Thomas Babington Macaulay made a case for establishing English as the medium of higher education in India, he argued not against the languages then spoken in the country, but against Sanskrit and Arabic, two languages already frozen into reverential antiquity and used mainly for religious instruction, championed only by maulavis, pandits and European scholars of Orientalism. The actual living languages were dismissed by Macaulay as 'dialects' and — by the use of his favourite rhetorical device of replacing logic by an assumption of universal agreement ('It seems to be admitted on all sides', 'I have never found one who would deny', 'It will hardly be disputed') — left out of the reckoning altogether:

All parties seem to be agreed on one point, that the dialects commonly spoken among the natives of this part of India contain neither literary nor scientific information, and are moreover, so poor and rude, that until they are enriched from some other quarter, it will not be easy to translate any valuable work into them.[3]

Yet within a generation these 'poor and rude' 'dialects' were creating vibrant literature, enriched undoubtedly by inputs made possible by the new education, and it is in these languages that the entire project of English in India is internalized, and also occasionally assessed and critiqued.

It is well known that English language and literature (Macaulay continued to emphasize the latter)[4] had a direct impact on the fiction and poetry that came to be written in the major Indian languages, but it is also in these texts that we find evidence of the ambivalence and self-reflexivity of Indian writers towards English, which was sometimes seen as a synecdoche for a whole way of life. I limit myself in this essay to the novel — a genre specific to the post-Macaulay generation in India, indirectly related to the exposure to English literature, but neither a simple transplantation nor the outcome of a 'total conquest', to use a category created by D.R. Nagaraj to describe different theories of colonization.[5] Those who work on the assumption of unilateral cultural conquest (for example, who take it for granted that British educational policy achieved its intended result) very often do not take into account the nineteenth-century archives available in the Indian languages — discursive or fictional. For example, the history of the novel in India alone can chart some of the complex negotiations between colonial education and its resistant impulses.

Novels began to be written in India during and after the crucial decade of the 1850s, marked on the one hand by the establishment of the three universities in Calcutta, Bombay and Madras by Acts II, XXII, and XXVIII of 1857, and on the other by the historic revolt in the same year, in the wake of which the rule of the East India

Company ended to herald the declaration of India as a British colony. Although only three years earlier Wood's Educational Despatch of 1854 had reiterated Macaulay's agenda by stating that the objective of higher education in India was 'the diffusion of the improved arts, sciences, philosophy and literatures of Europe',[6] there are indications that after the 1857 Revolt there was some rethinking among the British about the civilizing mission of education in India.[7] Unease about the education policy was couched in economic calculations of investment and return but there was an undercurrent of worry about its long-term political outcome. However, the process once set in motion could not be rolled back.

Novels from England became available in India in increasing numbers even if the intended readers were not primarily Indians. Priya Joshi in her detailed study on book imports in nineteenth-century India has shown that in 1863–4 books worth £3,28,024 were imported from England,[8] an enormous sum compared to the education bursary of £10,000 with which English education 'began' in India in 1835. Going through mid-nineteenth century issues of *The Calcutta Review, The Bombay Miscellany, Benares Recorder, Saturday Evening Harkaru,* journals written and consumed by Englishmen in India, one notices an anxiety about losing touch with the home country, to assuage which books were shipped out from England in large numbers. Out of these consignments, a sizeable percentage were contemporary novels of the popular variety, which eventually found their way to the homes of English- educated Indians who were otherwise encouraged in their curriculum to read only canonical texts. Traces of both, the prescribed novels and Victorian pulp, can be found in a curious amalgam in the early novels in the Indian languages.

The Watt who helps us to understand the beginnings of the novel in India is not Ian, but Sir James, the inventor of the steam engine. An anonymous article published in *The Calcutta Review* in 1846 extolled the virtue of steam — 'the mighty agent' that had brought about an 'intellectual revolution' in the subcontinent: 'Thanks to our splendid steamships ... every month brings to our shores a fresh supply of European literature, scarcely six weeks old.' (no. 9, 1846, p. 202)

These periodicals boosted the morale of the expatriates, telling them that they were not necessarily behind the country squire back home or 'the knowing citizen in London'. At a time in London when Thackeray was serializing *Vanity Fair* featuring Joseph Sedley — the caricature of a colonial figure — appearing to be provincial or comic in actual life might have been a real fear. Another editorial declared reassuringly: 'India is now part of England. We are very little out of the way: only six weeks behind our brothers and cousins in London, Exeter and Bath.'

Such indeed was the glory of steam in upholding British self-esteem.

But what effect did this spate of imported fiction have on its unintended readers — Indians who were now hungry for English books? While the Englishman in India was anxious about the contemporaneity of what he was reading — the later the better, the latest the best, six weeks being the minimum time lag he was compelled to suffer — the educated Indian saw all of western literature in a timeless continuum. His college curriculum exposed him simultaneously to several centuries of European classical texts and canonical literature from Britain, and 'colonial editions' of popular fiction of the time also became available to him outside the classroom. He responded to both enthusiastically and without much fastidiousness about literary status or chronology, although it is possible to detect a difference in the way such reading was processed by the Indian-language novelist and Indians who wrote novels in English.

Thus Lal Behari Day in his English novel *Govinda Samanta* (1874) refers to a Latin text, somewhat gratuitously, while describing a snake-bite in a Bengal village: '... it was not unlike those snakes in the forest of Calabria of which Virgil speaks in Georgics'. In another English novel Soshee Chunder Dutt quotes Longinus and Montaigne on the same page, while K.K. Sinha's novels (*The Star of Skiri*, 1893; and *Sanjogita or The Princess of Aryavarta*, 1903) are strewn with recognizable lines from Byron, Coleridge and Shakespeare, the author not always pausing to cite the source. While novelists in English were keen to display their familiarity with the best in western literature, Indian-language writers did not hesitate to acknowledge their debt to even low-brow writers like G.W.M. Reynolds, Edward Bulwer-Lytton and Benjamin Disraeli.[9]

The reception and assimilation of western literature in nineteenth-century India was complicated by several factors difficult to unravel from this distance in time. The new experience of being exposed to a different culture was so overwhelming and the events described in novels seemed so unreal and strange that it was possible to place all of it outside the axis of history. The response to poetry had a different dimension, as we can see from the following autobiographical account of Rabindranath Tagore in *Jibansmriti* (1912). He writes retrospectively of the 1880s in Calcutta when he was entering his twenties:

At that time English literature provided us with more intoxication than nourishment. Our literary gods were Shakespeare, Milton and Byron. What moved us most in their work was the predominance of passion, something that remained concealed in British social behaviour, but surfaced with intensity in literature. Excess of emotion culminating in a passionate explosion: this seemed the characteristic feature of this literature. At least what we learnt to think of as the quintessence of English literature was this unbridled passion ... the fury of King Lear's impotent lamentation, the all-consuming fire of Othello's jealousy — these contained an excess that fuelled our imagination.

Our society, all our petty spheres of work are hedged in by such dull enclosures that upheavals of heart have no way of entering there. These areas were as still and quiet as possible. Consequently, when the sudden velocity and violence of the heart's impulses as found in English literature struck us, it was a welcome jolt. The pleasure was not the aesthetic joy of literature; what appealed to us was the disturbance of the state of stagnation. Even if in the process slime from the bottom got churned up, it was acceptable.[10]

II

In the second half of the nineteenth century novels came to be written in India as much in Macaulay-maligned 'dialects' — or the so-called 'vernaculars' — as in English. While novels in Bangla, Marathi, Malayalam and other languages soon consolidated their strengths and initiated literary traditions that continue to this day, scores of English novels written in the late nineteenth and early twentieth century are virtually forgotten now. That English novels were written in considerable numbers during that period is a relatively recent discovery for me, because like most people in the field I used to believe that until the 1930s English writing in India was a freak phenomenon and that the sporadic books were to be regarded merely as historical curiosities. In 1995 I was asked to write an essay on these early novels for an *Illustrated History of Indian Literature in English*. Thus began my serendipitous journey of excavation in the National Library in Calcutta and other old libraries in the country, where I stumbled upon unexpected texts often too brittle to be photocopied, but fascinating for many reasons, specially in their attitude towards English literature, the Empire, nation, colonial modernity and the pre-colonial heritage. Although individually some of these novels may be deservedly forgotten, collectively they constitute a body of texts that cannot be ignored, and there are occasional gems among them crying out to be re-read from our end-century point of view. While the early novelists in the Indian languages are constantly being subjected to renewed critical assessments, their English counterparts have rarely been resuscitated for critical reading. Sales of books do not depend entirely on their intrinsic value; a complex concatenation of circumstances — not all of them literary — determine their trajectory in history. The reasons for this selective amnesia and the asymmetrical destinies of the English- and Indian-language novels of the colonial period need to be explored.

Within about twenty-five years after the passing of the Educational Minutes of 1835 which made English the official language of higher education in India, the new narrative form called the novel began to emerge, first in Bangla and Marathi (renamed *upanyas* and *kadambari*, respectively) to be followed soon after in Hindi, Urdu, Tamil and Malayalam. By the end of the century the novel became the most popular form of print-medium entertainment in at least eight major languages of the country. Also, the proliferation of literary periodicals in which these books were sometimes reviewed and discussed caused a sense of language-based cultural identity in the upper-caste elite families in urban areas — of which most men (but not the women) happened to be English-educated. Those who wrote novels in English also belonged to the same class, but for a long time their work was not perceived as mainstream literary activity in the country.

Shivarama Padikkal has argued that 'not all groups at all times produce artefacts which are classified as culture' and that 'literary production is one of the modes by which the dominant group constructs its reality and history'.[11] Since the writers of the English novels came from the most privileged strata of society, and by virtue of their proficiency in English occupied a position of dominance, by this logic their work should have gained a greater visibility in our literary history. Padikkal's statement is generally valid in the context of caste, class and gender hierarchies in our culture, but when it comes to language, perhaps certain other historical and geographical determinants also complicate the issues. In any case, the study of the early novel in India has to be much more than the textual examination of isolated texts. What became popular has to be seen in terms of extra-literary factors as well — not just issues of power and control, but also the emotional response to colonial education, simultaneously generating a sense of exhilaration and anxiety, the economics of journalism and publication, the attitude of the writers towards religion, community and regional identity — all generally related to the dynamics of social formation. The reality represented in the novel is not an unmediated reflection of what actually existed, but an ideological reconstruction moulded by an implicit political agenda in which language has, as I hope to demonstrate, a determining role.

A general belief about culture in colonial India — to which I have both subscribed and contributed in the past — is that among the early generations of English-educated Indians, those who were creative turned to their mother tongue, enriching these literatures by introducing new genres, poetic forms and narrative modes, while English became the language of public discourse, political mobilization and debates on social issues. The 'vernaculars' thus could be perceived as the repository of interiority and imagination, and English as a rational and functional tool for polemics and persuasion. But this formulation, I now realize, has only partial validity because it fails to take into account how English seeped into the intimate and personal domains of men of the elite classes — the class from which writers in all the languages emerged.

To support the earlier view (that the mother tongue was the natural vehicle of personal self-expression) two examples are frequently cited from nineteenth-century Bengal — that of Bankimchandra Chatterjee (1838–94) and Michael Madhusudan Dutt (1824–73), both of whom are supposed to have made 'false starts' by beginning their writing career in English, but realized this soon enough, made a switch and subsequently become famous as major writers in Bangla.[12] What is not mentioned is that even after they had discarded English in their creative writing, much of the personal correspondence of these writers continued in English. At the time when Michael Madhusudan was writing his famous

Bangla sonnet to declare his abandonment of this 'alien language',[13] he happened to be writing letters in English to his close friend Gourdas Basak, revealing his most intimate thoughts. Even his fear of being out of touch with his mother tongue needed to be conveyed in English. I quote from one of the many letters Michael Madhusudan wrote to Gourdas from Madras:

Can't you send me a copy of the Bengali translation of the Mahabhrut by Cassidos as well as a ditto of the Ramayana — Serampore edition. I am losing my Bengali faster than I can mention. Won't you oblige me, old friend, eh, Gour Das Bysack?[14]

In the western part of the country we find a later but similar example in the bilingualism of Govardhanram Tripathi. While writing his massive novel *Saraswatichandra* in Gujarati, he made extensive entries in English in his personal diaries, which he called his 'scrapbooks'. *Saraswatichandra* appeared in four volumes between 1887 and 1900 and gained immediate and immense popularity. While this was being written, the author scribbled some 1200 manuscript pages of introspective personal prose in English. In these pages many self-doubts were aired and a number of his private actions analysed philosophically, but the question of language was never mentioned — as if it was the most natural act to write a diary in English and a novel in Gujarati simultaneously. Even the editors of the 'scrapbooks' who published parts of these diary entries do not seem in any way to be concerned with this linguistic schizophrenia. In the Introduction they write:

In the scrapbooks an interested student will have full view of the thought processes of a great mind and a magnanimous heart, while in *Saraswatichandra* he will find these processes moulded into artistic forms.[15]

This complexity in the linguistic circumstances is indicated by the fact that Dutt and Tripathi use English in their interaction with close friends or dialogue with the self, but the artefact shaped for public consumption is presented in Bangla and Gujarati, respectively. English evidently was not the preferred language for literary recognition either regionally or nationally. Bankimchandra became well known in different parts of India through the Marathi, Kannada and Malayalam translations of his Bangla novels, while no one knew about or remembered his attempt to write a novel in English. In the early decades of the twentieth century another Bangla novelist, Saratchandra Chatterjee — who was hardly ever translated into English — enjoyed the same pan-Indian popularity through spontaneous and direct translation into various Indian languages.

When Romeshchandra Dutt (1848–1909), one of the earliest members of the Indian Civil Service and later remembered as the author of *The Economic History of India*, expressed his admiration and envy for Bankimchandra's Bangla writing, lamenting his own loss of his mother tongue, caused by his education in England, he was reprimanded by the elder writer. Bankim urged him to write in Bangla even if he was never formally trained in the language, insisting that whatever educated young men like him spoke could become the standard language when written down. He cited the negative examples of Govin Chunder Dutt and Soshee Chunder Dutt from Romesh's own family, whose talents, Bankim rightly predicted, would go unrecognized because they had chosen to write in English. Romeshchandra took this advice and went on to write six novels in Bangla (two of which he himself translated into English as *The Slave Girl of Agra* and *The Lake of Palms*) to gain considerable fame as a Bangla novelist. He continued to write discursive and scholarly prose in English and to translate from Sanskrit to English. He did not see any contradiction between his two careers.[16]

The best-known early novelists in India did not write in English, but their work carried traces of their reading of English fiction — some, like O. Chandu Menon acknowledge this debt gratefully — and there were numerous adaptations of popular Victorian novels in colonial India. More than a dozen widely-read novels in Bangla by Harisadhan Mukhopadhyay published between 1900 and 1920 and a similar number in Hindi by Kishorilal Goswami published between 1890 and 1913 were admittedly inspired by the success of W. M. Reynolds, whose *Mysteries of the Court of London* was a bestseller both in Hindi and Bangla translations as *London Rahasya*. Sometimes the influences were mediated through other Indian writers (e.g. the model of Sir Walter Scott's historical fiction got transmitted through Bankimchandra) and, curiously, in some instances the authors' prefaces were written in English even though the novel was not in English. A Kannada translation (1885) of Bankimchandra's *Durgeshnandini* (1866) carries a preface in English where the translator B. Venkatacharya quotes Edwin Arnold to gain validation for his own assessment of the value of the novel. There were writers like A. Madhavaiah who wrote novels both in Tamil and English, or translated their own work from one language to another, making it difficult for today's readers to separate their activities in two languages. From a recently published English translation of Lalitambika Anterjanam's (1909–85) Malayalam writing we know that in the early decades of the twentieth century she was deeply influenced not only by Rabindranath Tagore's Bangla novel *Ghare Baire* (1916) which she read in English as *Home and the Outside* serialized in *The Modern Review* (later it came to be titled *The Home and the World* in English) but also the fiction of a much less known Bangla writer Sitadebi Chattopadhyay.[17] Thus the interpellation of English in early Indian fiction happened in manifold exfoliating ways — operating through direct or indirect influences, translations, adaptations, as well as by acting as a bridge between different Indian languages.

III

Indian novels in English, a body of writing that has gained international visibility today, went virtually unnoticed in the nineteenth and early-twentieth century, and not necessarily because of numerical paucity or qualitative inferiority. There is a more complicated process at work here. Not all categories of writing at a given time get equal attention and enter into literary circulation. A particular configuration of circumstances creates a momentum that gets recorded in history. Why did the Indian novel in English fail to generate that momentum in the early years of the emergence of the novel in the subcontinent? A corollary to that would be another question, to be taken up later in this book: why are we witnessing a total reversal suddenly at the end of the twentieth century when an unmistakable and ebullient proliferation of fiction in English written by both resident and non-resident Indians has become a globally recognized and (consequently?) a nationally highlighted phenomenon? If in 1864 a Bankimchandra Chatterjee felt it necessary to discard his aspirations for a literary career in English, in 1995 we find a Kiran Nagarkar — trendsetting writer in Marathi — turning to writing in English. In neither case are the reasons arbitrary or strictly literary.

Literary texts get canonized in different and invidious ways — by being discussed and praised by influential critics, by being mentioned in histories of literature, by being taught in classrooms and through an accretion of commentary around them. Indian English novels of the nineteenth century have not been subjected to any of these canonizing processes, and have as a result been denied literary, historical or even archival value. Given the Indian apathy towards the preservation of stray documents from the past, and the high rate of paper disintegration in our climate, a good proportion of books that existed (often published privately by the author or by small presses with an inadequate distribution system) have perished beyond trace. Despite this, what survives in the National Library in Calcutta, the British Museum and the India Office Libraries in London, in old and obscure libraries around the country and in private collections of families, constitute no negligible archive.

Two facts stand out as one glances at the title pages of these
extant books. First, the diversity and range of places from where
these novels appeared — not only from the metropolitan centres
of book publication like Calcutta, Bombay and Madras (a few were
published from London) but also smaller places generally not
connected with publishing in English, like Allahabad, Bangalore,
Bezwada, Bhagalpur, Calicut, Dinapur, Midnapur, Surat or Vellore (see Appendix), indicating individual enterprise rather than
the support of an organized publication/distribution system; also
an absence of geographical cohesion, consequently of continuity
or tradition. Second, the eagerness in the titles to promise an
unveiling of some mystery ('A peep into', 'Glimpses of', 'Revelations', etc.) pertaining to a presumably homogeneous space called
India (or 'The East' or 'The Orient') inhabited by an undifferentiated 'Hindu' community ('A Story of Hindu Life', 'The Hindu
Wife'). This tendency was inextricably linked with the language
authors wrote in, because unlike the novelists in Bangla, Marathi
or Malayalam, who were confident about a sizeable readership
within their specific geographic region, the writer in English
suffered from an uncertainty about his audience. From clues embedded in the text, the implicit addressee seemed to be situated
outside the culture, possibly in England, or among colonial administrators living in India who were concrete representatives of
the abstract Other as far as Indians were concerned. This does not
necessarily mean that these people were the actual consumers of
this fiction. Following Susie Tharu's general formulation about
the addresser's discursive relationship about the addressee, one
could argue that even in this specific case

(T)hough the addresser and the addressee are assumed to be prior to and
independent of the discourse, in other words, as "already there", both
these figures are not only positioned, but also constructed by the logic
of the discourse, they are its producers.[18]

We watch this shadowy addressee being constructed in these

English novels through details of ethnographic documentation or in explanatory asides or semantic or lexical shifts. For example when Lal Behari Day in his novel *Govinda Samanta* (1874) announces without any context that there are no taverns in Bengal villages for peasants to spend an evening in, or that young men and women in India have no concept of courtship, he is testifying to his concern with an alien reader. His gratuitous cultural gloss goes on to elaborate matters for the benefit of this reader:

In Bengal — and in most of India — they do not make love in the honourable sense of that word. Unlike the butterfly whose courtship Darwin assures us, is a very long affair, the Bengali does not court at all. Marriage is an affair arranged either by the parents and guardians of the bachelors and the spinsters. (p. 3)

A. Madhavaiah in his novel *Satyananda* (1909) similarly pauses in his narration to provide anthropological details about the outlandish habits of Hindus:

The Hindu husband and his wife have no recognised form of addressing each other and strange are the devices often resorted to by them ... The Brahman wife generally calls her lord's attention by means of a peculiar noise ... while the husband refers to his helpmate as "she", "it", "our housewoman", "you" or more often by a meaningless interjection. (p. 255)

In all these instances, and the examples could easily be multiplied, we perceive how the addresser is in turn being constructed by the supposed addressee. The indeterminacy of this discursive relationship has ambiguous effects on the way the author positions himself in the text. At a time when one of the indirect functions of the Indian language novel was the consolidation of an incipient nationalism of the pan-Indian as well as regional variety, the writers in English were careful not to antagonize their imagined addressee through overtones of sedition. The language, English, ruled out any possibility of a regional identity, and any assertion of a broadly *Indian* identity was undertaken generally to emphasize otherness and exoticity rather than to make a political statement. Even an explosive theme like the Revolt of 1857 is completely de-politicized in Soshee Chunder Dutt's novel *Shunker* (1885) set against this historical backdrop. The author takes special care to distribute sympathy evenly between the British and Indians. If officers like Bernard and Mackenzie are presented as despicable creatures ready to rape the Indian woman who gave them shelter, Nanasaheb's treachery and promiscuity are highlighted as if to provide a balance in villainy. There is an implicit anxiety to uphold the ordinary Indian soldier's loyalty to the Crown. Occasional insurgency is projected as a temporary reaction to the injustice and ill-treatment of individual officers. Shunker's vendetta against those who raped his wife is made out to be a purely personal matter, with no political or racial implication whatsoever.

Soshee Chunder Dutt's longer novel *The Young Zamindar* (1883) does describe resistance movements against the British in different parts of India, seen through the eyes of Manohar, the young zamindar, and his mentor Babaji Bissonath, an ascetic, who together travel across the country, but only to come to the conclusion that due to lack of discipline and an absence of leadership such attempts are destined to fail. At the end of the novel Manohar accepts British presence in the country as inevitable and beneficial. While in most of Bankimchandra Chatterjee's Bangla novels we find that the occasional Englishman who makes his appearance is either the abductor or the adversary (e.g. Laurence Foster in *Chandrashekhar*, Captain Thomas in *Anandamath* and the Lieutenant Saheb in *Debi Chaudhurani*), in his solitary English novel *Rajmohan's Wife* the white man is ascribed a positive function and the justice and efficiency of the British rule is unequivocally, if briefly, proclaimed at the end.

By the turn of the century, when the novel in the 'vernaculars' had become a major vehicle of political dissent, positing in fictional terms what was not yet feasible in the arena of action, novel after novel in English paid direct or veiled tribute to imperial rule. A historical novel by K.K. Sinha titled *Sanjogita or The Princess of Aryavarta* (1903) describing the defeat of Prithvi Raj Chauhan by Mohammad Ghori as caused by internal dissension and a lack of vision — a situation clearly parallel to the British takeover of India — completely elided the present colonial moment to go into a nostalgic evocation of the greatness of the Hindu past. But suddenly towards the end of the novel there is an unceremonious switch to a different rhetoric:

India appeals to her noble foreign masters for kindness and sympathy; she is indebted to them for her rescue from a chaotic society. (p. 267)

This abject servility coexists easily with a fierce cultural pride and frequent assertions of the antiquity and superiority of Hindu civilization in relation to Europe. Recounting the saga of the princely state of Barathpur (clearly an allegory for India) Sarath Kumar Ghosh, the author of *Prince of Destiny or The New Krishna* (1909) wrote:

When Rome was not built, when Tyre and Carthage were yet unbegotten, the house of Bharath reigned supreme over India. (p. 20)

Similarly, the author of *Sanjogita* proudly claimed in his Preface: 'Long before Pythagorus was born in Athens, the theory of transmigration of souls was known to the Hindu people.' Conflation of the words 'Brahman' and 'Hindu', and also 'Hindu' with 'India', was a common practice based on an assumption that the entire range of these terms evoked a civilizational essence.[19] Not only the English novels but also novels in the Indian languages of the same period often participated in this assumption. What Frantz Fanon in a different context has described as the coloured man's desire to prove to white men the richness of his thought and experience[20] becomes a distinctly pronounced trait in the English novels whose authors probably envisaged a largely foreign readership for their work. The repeated though marginal figure of a spiritual mentor figure — a guru or a saffron-clad ascetic — in many of these novels serves the dual function of proclaiming the wisdom and spirituality of the ancient Hindu civilization and admitting at the same time its ineffectuality in the colonial domain of action and power.

IV

The early novelists in the 'vernacular' and the novelists in English belonged to roughly the same social segment across the country — upper-caste urban Hindu male (women like Swarnakumari Debi or Krupa Satthianadhan were rare exceptions) and must have read the same English books — both canonical and popular. Yet the language in which they wrote seemed to automatically determine the way this reading would be processed for creative purposes. Indian English novelists displayed their acquaintance with the classics of western literature more readily than did Indian-language novelists, parading this knowledge as validation, as it were, of their status in the eyes of the putative reader. They never mentioned the popular writers except to denounce them,[21] and took care to align themselves only with the best in ingenious ways. Using epigraphs from Byron, Scott, Cowper, Moore, Shakespeare or Coleridge at the beginning of chapters was a common practice; quotations and references were generously woven in whether the narrative called for them or not; veiled allusions were left unexplained in the hope that the reader would recognize them. The community of imagined readers was expected to be bound by this specialized literary knowledge — which, apart from the target group of outsiders, might also have meant to include some Indian men as highly educated as themselves, but excluded Indian women almost totally.

This issue of gender is a major factor in the differential trajectories of these two sets of novels: in English and in the Indian languages. Knowledge of English was a gender-specific skill in nineteenth-century India. Although women's education was one of the issues in the social reform movement, the debates focused more on what and how much they should be taught, rather than whether they should be taught English. It was assumed both in Bengal and Maharashtra that women were best instructed through the mother tongue. One of the strengths of the novel in the Indian languages was the fact that its intended readership contained a sizeable percentage of women. It is well known that *Indulekha* (1889), one of the early novels in Malayalam, was professedly written for a woman who had no access to the new form of entertainment called the novel, popular among English-knowing Malayali men. O. Chandu Menon wanted to recreate the genre in Malayalam both for the entertainment of women and also to set up an idealized model of modernity for Nair women. In the absence of concrete data one cannot speak too confidently about the proportion of women among the readers of fiction in these early years, but judging from the authors' asides or the assumptions in the narratives, they were not a negligible minority. We also know that as early as 1858 a women's magazine had started in Gujarati (*Sundari Subodh*) and *Bamabodhini Patrika*, a similar magazine in Bangla, was established in 1863. By the 1880s at least two other women's journals — *Bangamahila* and *Paricharika* — were appearing from Calcutta.[22] A satirical sketch in a Bangla journal in 1878 in the form of a dialogue between a husband and a wife sums up some of the attitudes on gender and language as far as the novel was concerned. In reply to the English-educated husband's inquiry about what she is reading, the wife replies:

I know neither your English nor your French. I read whatever is available to me.
  Why do you waste time reading this Bangla trash? It is better not to read anything than read this stuff.
  But why?
  Because these books are immoral, obscene and filthy.[23]

Incidentally, the husband has to use the last three words in English because his education has made him forget the Bangla equivalents. By the end of the conversation the husband emerges clearly as the butt of the joke because his wife is not only familiar with many Bangla novels but has also read more English books in Bangla adaptation than her husband has read in the original. The English-educated young man who disparaged his mother tongue was a recurrent figure or ridicule, while the woman reader became the touchstone of authenticity in the Bangla literary discourse of the period.

Novels in English hardly ever provide us with examples of self-reflexivity about the language they use, enclosed as they are generally within the cognitive and cultural limits of their linguistic medium. The only exception I have found is *Govinda Samanta* where the author apologizes for making the uneducated Bengal peasant speak standard English:

Gentle reader, allow me here to make one remark. You perceive that Badan and Alanga speak better English than most uneducated English peasants; they speak almost like educated ladies and gentlemen without any provincialisms. But how could I have translated their talk into the Somersetshire or the Yorkshire dialect? I would have then turned them into English, and not Bengali peasants. (p. 61)

The claim that the author could have used any of the dialects of England if he wanted (he simply chooses not to, for the sake of authenticity) rings hollow because an educated Indian hardly had so much manoeuvrability in his carefully learnt text-based language. In the rest of the novel language acquires a transparency for Day, who never admits to any other problem about rendering life in a Bengal village in English.

We have to turn to the texts of the Indian languages to understand how the complex function of English was perceived in the culture. On the one hand a command of English conferred marks of class and privilege on the fictional characters, adding to their image of a superior masculinity as in the case of the eponymous hero in Rabindranath Tagore's *Gora* (1909). Gora's uniqueness however is predicated upon the unusual combination of skill in English writing and oratory with Hindu Brahmanic orthodoxy. On the other hand English was also seen as a language that estranged men from their social matrix. In another Tagore novel, *Chaturanga*, an acknowledged master of English is described with a touch of acerbic wit:

Some hailed him as the Macaulay of Bengal, others regarded him as the Johnson of this century. Like the shell of a tortoise his life was encased in English books.[24]

The simile of the tortoise underlines the insulating function of English, removing the man who internalizes it from whatever is not cerebral or sophisticated. The epithets celebrating his eminence — 'Macaulay of Bengal', etc. — make him out to be a replica of some other model, not an original himself. As a contrast, the women — outside the magic circle of English — are perceived as natural and in touch with the reality of felt experience. This opposition gets further concretized in another narrative, also by Tagore: *Nashtaneer* (translated into English as *The Broken Nest* and titled *Charulata* in Satyajit Ray's film version). Here the husband and the wife stand as it were on two sides of the language divide. The husband Bhupati who does not need to work in order to earn money feels compelled nevertheless to publish an English-language newspaper because:

Ever since childhood he had enjoyed writing and making speeches in English. Even when they were uncalled for he wrote letters in English-language papers, and even if he had nothing to say, he left no public gathering without saying a few words (in English).[25]

This infatuation with English created a distance between him and his domestic and cultural moorings. His wife Charu, on the other hand, not having any literary training either in Sanskrit or English

— the two poles of high culture — draws upon the experience of her rural childhood to write simple but moving pieces for Bangla journals which are not only published but much appreciated. By the end of the novel the husband is adrift, his newspaper project has floundered economically; he cannot make his way back either to his wife or to his mother tongue. In the final pages of the novel, Bhupati, in a bid to come closer to his wife tries to read and translate Tennyson for her, but it does not work. 'He could not find exact Bangla equivalents for words. Charu's vacant look told him that she was not attentive.'[26]

The implicit valorization of Bangla as the language of natural-ness and authenticity of which women were the custodians con-solidated the inside–outside dichotomy that has been posited by Partha Chatterjee more than a decade ago — the separation of the interior as sacral space uncontaminated by the West and woman as its preserver. The Indian languages capitalized on the emotional resonance of this unspoken assumption by invoking regional na-tionalism through the merger of gender and language. The figure of 'Banga-janani' embodied both language and land and there were similar constructions in other parts of the country as well. Shiva-rama Padikkal has argued that 'the most significant motivating force behind the early Kannada novels [was] the search for a Kannadaness ... In the novels we begin to find the god-like figure of the Kannada matha [the Kannada-mother].'[27] The figure of Kairali which combines the language Malayalam and the land of Kerala, or the line of the popular song by Shankarambadi Sun-daracharya in Andhra Pradesh 'ma telugu thalliki malle pu danda' (to our Telugu mother a garland of jasmine) are examples of the continuing valency of these composite images in different linguis-tic regions.

Language-centred nationalism and the concept of a nation that transcends linguistic divisions reinforced each other in this period and the novel in India emerged at the cusp of these twin impulses.

One without the other could not have sustained a genre that served a complex function in a colonial society, providing a vehicle for the emergence of political aspirations, imaginative adventure, historical reconstruction as well as a desire to document contemporary life. The novel as well as Indian nationalism stand at the conjunction of English — which not only opened out a new literary horizon but introduced new knowledge — and the Indian languages which became the conduit for processing this knowledge to suit regional needs. Why these needs were dissimilar — that is, why novels in Bangla, Marathi and Tamil happened to evolve differently despite early British presence in the three coastal cities and the simultaneous establishment of universities, what mutual variations in the gravitational pulls of earlier knowledge systems, cultural productions and social formations affected their diverse ways of responding to the colonial impact — would be an area for separate research, but for the present essay it suffices that the novels in all these languages were equally distant from the novels in English written at that time by those who lived in the same region.

The Indian novel in English during the colonial era had no way of drawing sustenance from this particular configuration of the regional and the national mentioned above, in which the role of gender was crucial, and that could be one of the reasons why this body of writing was destined to reach a dead end at that time. It took the genre in English nearly another century to come into its own in a post-colonial dispensation and a globalized economy. Thomas de Quincey had made a claim for the English language in 1862 which had seemed like wishful thinking at that time: 'The English language is travelling fast towards the fulfilment of its destiny ... running forward towards its ultimate mission of eating up, like Aaron's rod, all other languages.'[28] Paradoxically this destiny seems nearer to fulfilment now at the end of the millennium than ever before, while during the heyday of imperial rule, despite the overwhelming presence of English literature in the curriculum of higher education, the English language remained quite peripheral in the literary agenda of the country.

Notes

1. 'Kono specialer patra', *Bankim Rachanabali*, ed. Jogeshchandra Bagal (Calcutta: Sahitya Sansad, 1954), vol. II, p. 32, my translation.

2. 'Bangala bhasha', ibid., pp. 368–74.

3. Thomas Babington Macaulay, 'Minutes on Indian Education', *Victorian Prose*, ed. S. Nagarajan *et al.* (Poona: University of Poona Publication, 1968), p. 69.

4. In 1846 in a speech before the Edinburgh Philosophical Society, Macaulay offered a toast

> (T)o the literature of Britain ... which has exercised an influence wider than that of our commerce and mightier than that of our arms ... before the light of which impious and cruel superstitions are fast taking flight on the banks of the Ganges.

The Works of Lord Macaulay: Speeches and Poems with the Reports and Notes on the Indian Penal Code (New York: Riverside Press, 1867), pp. 40–1.

5. It is possible to identify three streams in the existing theories of colonialism: the schools that are defined by the idea of total conquest, the ones that are organized around the idea of a cultural soul, and the ones that stress mutual transformation. The first is represented by the likes of Frantz Fanon, Albert Memmi and Edward Said, the second by the likes of Ananda Coomaraswamy and Seyyed Hossein Nasr, the third by Nandy.

D.R. Nagaraj in the Introduction to *Exiled at Home* by Ashis Nandy (Delhi: Oxford University Press, 1998), p. xxiii.

From the point of view of English Studies I am tempted to add the name of Gauri Viswanathan to the first category and of Harish Trivedi to the third.

6. Quoted in *Indian Journal of History of Science*, vol. 23, nos 3 and 4 (July and October 1988), pp. 311–12.

7. This can be surmised from some of the post-mutiny documents of the time. For example, in a letter dated 28 April 1859, addressed by the President of the Board of Control to the Chairman and Deputy Chairman of the East India Company in which the unwarranted expenditure of 'a rapidly progressive character' caused by the education policy was severely criticized. The second example is a memorandum by Sir G.R. Clerk, Secretary of the Board,

forwarded by Lord Ellenborough to the Board of Directors, which opposed a policy that 'was teaching the natives only to babble in English' and encouraged cramming. Both documents are quoted in *Indian Journal of History of Science*, ibid.

8. Priya Joshi, 'Culture and Consumption: Fiction, the Reading Public and the British Novel in Colonial India', *Book History* I: 1, 1998, pp. 196–220.

9. For example, Hari Narain Apte modelled one of his novels on *The Seamstress*, a Victorian bestseller by G.W.M. Reynolds; Bankimchandra acknowledged his debt to Bulwer-Lytton and Wilkie Collins in the Preface to his novel *Rajani*; O. Chandu Menon similarly mentioned Benjamin Disraeli's *Henrieta Temple* in the preface to *Indulekha*. For more examples see my earlier study *Realism and Reality: The Novel and Society in India* (Delhi: Oxford University Press, 1984).

10. 'Jibansmriti', *Rabindra Rachanabali* (125th Birth Centenary Edition), vol. IX, p. 478, my translation.

11. Shivarama Padikkal, 'Inventing Modernity: The Emergence of the Novel in India', *Interrogating Modernity: Culture and Colonialism in India*, eds. Tejaswini Niranjana, P. Sudhir and Vivek Dhareshwar (Calcutta: Seagull Books, 1893), p. 220.

12. Bankimchandra Chatterjee's first novel was written in English (*Rajmohan's Wife*, 1864, which is discussed separately in an essay later in this book), and after that he wrote all his novels in Bangla. Michael Madhusudan's first published book was a long narrative poem, 'The Captive Ladie', 1849. His Bangla career began nearly ten years later.

13. A rough prose paraphrase of Dutt's sonnet is given below:

> O Bengal, your treasury is full of various gems. Ignoring them I foolishly travelled abroad, infatuated with the wealth of others. I spent long unhappy days without food or sleep striving to achieve what was not worth striving for. Forgetting the lotus garden I trudged through moss and slime. Then *kula-lakshmi* appeared in my dream and said: "When your mother's store is full of treasure, why do you roam around like a beggar? Go back, ignorant one, go home." I obeyed her and discovered in time the wealth of my mother tongue, replete with precious jewels.

Sonnet 3, 'Chaturdashpadi Kabitabali', *Madhusudan Rachanabali*, ed. Kshetra Gupta (Calcutta: Sahitya Sansad, 1965), p. 159.

14. Ibid. Quoted in the Introduction, p. xvi. The orthography of Madhusudan (Kossidas for Kashidas, Bysak for Basak, etc.) seems quite unique today. For more comments on nineteenth-century spelling of Indian names see note 34 (pp. 128–9) to the essay titled 'Hearing Her Own Voice'.

15. Govardhanram Tripathi, *Scrapbook 1888–1894*, ed. Kantilal C. Pandya, Ramprasad P. Bakshi and Sanmukhlal J. Pandya (Bombay: N.M. Tripathi Pvt. Ltd., 1959), vol. I, p. xiv.

16. Romeshchandra Dutt wrote six novels in Bangla: *Bangabijeta* (1874), *Madhabikankan* (1877), *Maharashtra Jiban Prabhat* (1878), *Rajput Jiban Sandhya* (1879), *Sansar* (1886) and *Samaj* (1894) apart from many essays on literature, religion, philosophy and economics published in different Bangla journals. His English works (eighteen titles in all) range from *Three Years in Europe* (1872), *The Peasantry of Bengal* (1974) to *A History of Civilization of Ancient India* (3 vols) (1888–90) to *Economic History of India* (2 vols), 1902 and 1904.

17. Lalitambika Anterjanam, *Cast Me Out If You Will: Stories and Memoirs*, translated by Gita Krishnankutty (Calcutta: Stree, 1998), p. 53.

18. Susie Tharu, 'Government, Binding and Unbinding: Alienation and the Subject of Literature', *Subject to Change: Teaching Literature in the Nineties*, ed. Susie Tharu (Hyderabad: Orient Longman, 1998), p. 10.

19. Even as late as 1961 we find the same brahmanic definition of India in Raja Rao's *The Serpent and the Rope*.

20. Frantz Fanon, *Black Skin, White Masks* (1950; London: Pluto Press, 1986), p. 12.

21. The hero of A. Madhavaiah's *Thillai Govindan* describes his progress thus: 'I was always fond of books, and when Reynolds was discarded, Scott, Thackeray, Dickens and George Eliot took his place', p. 160.

22. These dates are culled from *A History of Indian Literature*, vol. VIII, Sisir Kumar Das (Delhi: Sahitya Akademi, 1991) and *Andare Antare: Unish Shatake Bangali Bhadramahila*, Sambudhha Chakrabarty (Calcutta: Stree, 1995).

23. 'Bangala Sahityer Ador', *Bankim Rachanabali*, vol. II, pp. 44–6.

24. 'Chaturanga', *Rabindra Rachanabali*, vol. IV, p. 427, my translation.

25. 'Nashtaneer', *Rabindra Rachanabali*, vol. XI, p. 362.

26. Ibid., p. 410.

27. Shivarama Padikkal, p. 220.

28. Thomas de Quincey, 'Recollections of the Lakes and the Lake Poets', 1862, *Complete Works of de Quincey*, vol. II (Edinburgh: Adams & Charles Black, 1889), p. 268.

APPENDIX
Early Fiction in English 1830–1930
(chronologically arranged)

Dutt, Kylas Chunder. *A Journal of Forty Eight Hours of the Year 1945.* Published in *The Calcutta Literary Gazette*, June 1835.

Dutt, Soshee Chunder. *The Republic of Orissa: A Page from the Annals of the 20th Century.* First published in *The Saturday Evening Harakuru*, May 1845. Later included in *Bengaliana: A Dish of Rice and Curry and Other Indigestible Ingredients*, Calcutta, 1885.

Khan, Panchkouree. *The Revelations of an Orderly.* First published in *Benares Recorder*, 1846 (?). Subsequent editions: London, 1849; Calcutta, 1857; Calcutta, 1891.

Chatterjee, Bankimchandra. *Rajmohan's Wife.* Serialized in *Indian Field*, 1864. Subsequent editions: Calcutta, 1935, Brajendra Nath Banerjee (ed.); Calcutta, 1969, Jogeshchandra Bagal (ed.), *Bankim Rachanabali*, vol. III; New Delhi, 1996, Meenakshi Mukherjee (ed.).

Punt, Ram Krishna. *The Boy of Bengal.* London and Philadelphia, 1866.

Mookerjee, Tarachand. *The Scorpion of Eastern Thoughts.* Allahabad, 1868.

Dutt, Soshee Chunder. *Reminiscences of A Kerani's Life.* Serialized in *Mookerjee's Magazine* in 1873. Later included in *Bengaliana*, Calcutta, 1885.

Day, Lal Behari. *Govinda Samanta* or *The History of a Bengali Raiyat.* London, 1874. Revised and enlarged version published as *Bengal Peasant Life*, London, 1908.

Debi, Rajlakshmi. *The Hindu Wife or The Enchanted Fruit.* Calcutta, 1878.

Dutt, Toru. *Bianca: Or The Young Spanish Maiden.* Serialized in *The Bengal Magazine*, January–April 1878.

Dutt, Soshee Chunder. *The Young Zamindar*, 3 volumes. London, 1883.

Alee Beg (Gaekwaree), Mirza Moorad. *Lalun, the Beragan: Or the Battle of Paniput: A Legend of Hindoostan*, 2 volumes. Bombay, 1884.

Das, Trailokya Nath. *Hirimba's Wedding.* Midnapur, 1884.

Dutt, Soshee Chunder. *Shunkur: A Tale of the Indian Mutiny of 1857.* London, 1885.

Chattopadhyay, Yogendranath. *The Girl and Her Tutor.* Bhagalpur, 1891.

Sinha, K.K. *The Star of Sikri*. Dinapur, 1893.

Satthianadhan, Krupabai. *Kamala, A Story of Hindu Life*. Madras and Bombay, 1895.

—— *Saguna, A Story of Native Christian Life*. Madras and Bombay, 1895.

Nikambe, Shevantibai M. Ratanbai. *A Sketch of Bombay High Caste Hindu Young Wife*. London, 1895.

Rajam Iyer, B.R. *True Greatness, or Vasudeva Sastri*. Serialized in Prabuddha Bharata 1896–8. Later published as a book, London, 1925.

Chakravarti, Kshetrapal. *Sarala and Hingana*. Calcutta, 1899.

Pillai, T. Ramakrishna. *Padmini*. London, 1903.

Sinha, K.K. *Sanjogita or The Princess of Aryavarta*. Dinapur, 1903.

Pal, L.B. *A Glimpse of Zanana Life in Bengal*. Calcutta, 1904.

Ghosh, Sarath Kumar. *Verdict of the Gods*. London, 1906.

Madhavaiah, A. *Thillai Govindan*. First published in India 1908 (?). Later edition London, 1916.

Ghosh, Sarath Kumar. *The Prince of Destiny: The New Krishna*, London, 1909.

Mitra, S.M. *Hindupur: A Peep Behind the Indian Unrest: An Anglo-Indian Romance*. London, 1909.

Madhavaiah, A. *Satyananda*. Bangalore, 1909.

Banerjea, S.B. *The Adventures of Mrs Russel*. London, 1909.

Singh, Sirdar Jogendra. *Nur Jahan, The Romance of an Indian Queen*. London, 1909.

Bal Krishna. *The Love of Kusuma: An Eastern Love Story*. London, 1910.

Singh, Sirdar Jogendra. *Nasrin, an Indian Medley*. London, 1911.

Pillai, T. Ramakrishna. *A Dive for Death*. London, 1911.

Munshi, M.M. *Beauty and Joy*. Surat, 1914.

Rau, Srinivasa. *Varanasi: The Portuguese Ambassador*. Bezwada, 1914.

Madhavaiah, A. *Clarinda*. Madras, 1915.

Panikkar, T.K. Gopal. *Storm and Sunshine*. Calicut, 1916.

Parthsarathy, C. *Sangili Karuppam or The Wheel of Destiny*. Vellore, 1920.

Singh, Sirdar Jogendra. *Kamla*. London, 1925. [This author's next — and last — novel *Kamini* (Lahore, 1931) falls outside the period covered in this bibliography.]

Venkataramani, K.S. *Murugan, the Tiller*. London, 1927. [The author's only other novel *Kandan, the Patriot* (Madras, 1934) falls outside the period covered in this bibliography.]

Chintamani, V.V. *Vedantam: The Clash of Traditions*, London, 1928.

Chinna Durai, J. *Sugirtha: An Indian Novel*. London, 1929.

Ayyar, A.S.P. *Baladitya*, 1929. [The author's only other novel *Three Men of Destiny* (1939) falls outside the period covered in this bibliography.]

Narain, Ram. *The Tigress of the Harem*. New York, 1930.

2

Rajmohan's Wife:
The First Indian English Novel

Sometime in 1864, a twenty-six year old Deputy Magistrate posted in Khulna district (Bengal Presidency) wrote a novel in English called *Rajmohan's Wife*. It was serialized in a short-lived weekly magazine published from Calcutta, but did not appear as a book in the author's lifetime. As the first Indian novel in English, *Rajmohan's Wife* has for well over a century been a text more heard of than read.

This early fictional work of Bankimchandra Chatterjee/Chattopadhyaya (1838–94) was subsequently overshadowed by the fourteen novels he wrote in Bangla, including *Durgeshnandini* (1865), *Anandamath* (1882), and *Rajsingha* (1893) which were widely read, emulated, discussed and translated into other Indian languages. *Rajmohan's Wife* never had that kind of visibility, partly because the book was not easily accessible, but also because most commentators and critics of Bankimchandra regarded his foray into English writing as 'a false start' after which he is supposed to have found his true metier in Bangla.

Read today, after 130 years of its first appearance, *Rajmohan's Wife* remains a fascinating text for a number of reasons. In India, the novel as a genre was in its infancy in 1864 and, while romance was acceptable as a narrative mode, there was no precedent as yet of mimetic rendering of domestic life in fiction, or of weaving a plot out of contemporary social and familial situations. Yet *Rajmohan's Wife* is very nearly realistic in its representation of East Bengal middle-class life. The story of the beautiful and passionate Matangini married to a villainous man is astonishingly rich in details in the depiction of interiors and the quotidian routine of women's lives. It goes beyond realism in the evocative use of nature — as, for example in the account of Matangini's secret journey through a dark and stormy night, which uses the descriptive conventions of Vaishnava love poetry, and in anticipating several of Bankimchandra's more mature novels where landscape and nature are employed as narrative motifs.

There is also an attempt in *Rajmohan's Wife* to foreground the ways in which the home and the world are inextricably linked, a relationship which also happened to be of some concern to the classic realist novelists of nineteenth-century Europe, by locating the drama within the conjugal and domestic space in relation to the external arena of property, legality, crime and the colonial administration. Inscribed in the text we also find an early statement about the helplessness and claustrophobia of women in incompatible marriages that was to be a recurrent concern in Indian fiction for many years to come. Given the rigidity of the power structure within the family among upper-caste Bengalis in the nineteenth century, it seems surprising that the first Indian novel in a contemporary setting should have focused on a woman of uncommon vitality who refused to be completely subjugated either by her brutal husband or by the expectations of society. Matangini's unrequited love for her own sister's husband is presented with authorial sympathy, but the abruptness and the ambivalence of the ending may be the result of anxiety that such women of energy generated by posing a threat to the social order and creating a moral dilemma for the author.

The other aspect of the novel that specially intrigues us today is the language. Now, in the last decade of the twentieth century, when many more Indians are writing in English than ever before, we are so accustomed to this literary phenomenon that we seldom pause to reflect on why, and for which audience, a Bengali or a Marathi or a Tamil writer should want to write in English. When Bankimchandra, who was in the first graduating batch of the newly-founded Calcutta University, began to write *Rajmohan's Wife*, he must have known that the English-reading population of Bengal was not very widespread. Did he visualize clearly who was going to be his reader? The half-hearted attempts at textual explanations of cultural details suggest a vague awareness of readers who may be outsiders to the Bengali way of life — possibly the British administrators in India — but given the historical circumstances and the place of publication, this could not have comprised a sizeable readership. His subsequent decision of never again writing fiction in English may have had as much to do with his realization of the illusory nature of his audience as with his nationalist ideology, or his honest artistic self-appraisal. In *Rajmohan's Wife* Bankimchandra's attempt to negotiate the semantic and connotative hurdles that are involved in rendering an Indian (in this case Bengali) ethos in the English language, without any previous model whatsoever, forces us to think about the interconnectedness of culture and language, narrative voice and implied readership — issues that have not ceased to be relevant. It also makes us go beyond literary questions about how well one writes in English to non-literary enquiries regarding the publication, distribution and marketing of a literary product in the local, national or global market. It is indeed worth considering the complex circumstances that made Bankimchandra shift from English to the mother-tongue before he could gain national recognition, while in late twentieth-century India the process may well get reversed.

II

After *Rajmohan's Wife* (1864), Bankimchandra Chatterjee abandoned his creative project in English altogether and went on to write novels and discursive prose in Bangla, which made him not only the most prominent literary figure of nineteenth-century Bengal, but a major protagonist in India's intellectual history, one who continues to be vigorously read, interpreted and debated upon even a century after his death. Quite apart from the vast quantities of commentaries on Bankimchandra's work that exist in Bangla, in the last decade or so several historians and literary scholars have begun to write on him in English.[1] They demonstrate how Bankimchandra's novels serve as productive sites for studying the complex, and often contradictory, configurations of the colonial mind, as also for understanding the process in which the emergent notion of national identity was constructed through fictional re-writings of history. His Bangla novels, those set in the past as well as in his own time, are constantly being reinterpreted and deconstructed from new perspectives — for example, feminist theory or colonial discourse — to unravel new layers of meaning, and even the silences and ellipses in the text are made to reveal cultural anxieties.

But his only novel in English has left behind no such wake. We have no evidence of what his contemporary readers thought of the novel, or whether anyone read it at all in the century that followed. Those interested in the history of Indian writing in English know about the existence of the novel, but even for them it has been little more than a dead entry carried over from one bibliography to another, without anyone trying to exhume the corpse, or attempting to perform a post-mortem. Even those critics who made dismissive references to the novel, designating it as 'a false start', seldom took the trouble to explain what exactly was wrong with it.[2]

When Bankimchandra died in 1894, his younger contemporary Aurobindo Ghose (later Sri Aurobindo) wrote a series of seven commemorative pieces on him in a Bombay based journal, *Induprakash*, in which he casually mentioned this novel but only as evidence to prove his favourite thesis: 'To be original in an acquired language is hardly feasible.' According to Ghose (who himself, incidentally, only wrote in English), for an Indian the enterprise of writing in English had 'something unnatural and spurious about it — like speaking with a stone in the mouth or walking with stilts'.[3] Bankimchandra's English novel seems to have inspired little critical observation beyond such sweeping assertions. Out of the seventy-five essays included in the massive 700-page centenary volume *Bankimchandra: Essays in Perspective* published by the Sahitya Akademi in 1994, not one focuses on *Rajmohan's Wife*, and the few incidental references to it found in the pages of this book merely reiterate opinions expressed in the past.[4]

III

Rajmohan's Wife was Bankim's initial and tentative attempt to write fiction based on a Victorian narrative model to which colonial education had exposed a new generation of urban Indians. Independently, similar attempts were being made in several Indian languages in the second half of the nineteenth century. Although literary historians have cited different and contesting dates for the first Indian novel, it may be safe to say that when *Rajmohan's Wife* was written, the novel was still a new and malleable genre in India. Only two years after his still-born English text Bankim wrote his first work of fiction in Bangla, *Durgeshnandini* (1866), whose success was resounding, and the reverberations continued for several decades: the novel was reprinted, dramatized and emulated in Bangla repeatedly and was subsequently translated or adapted in several other Indian languages. Set in the late sixteenth century,

Durgeshnandini depicts the conflict between a Mughal emperor of Delhi and his subedar in Bengal, evoking the extravagance, colour and the imaginative intensity of a romance. The romance mode, blended with history, continued to be a dominant strand in the narrative fiction of several Indian languages — in Bangla, Hindi and Marathi, for example — till the end of the nineteenth century.

Rajmohan's Wife, which predates Bankim's success in the romance mode, had attempted a realistic representation of contemporary Bengali life, modified no doubt by the pulls of other narrative traditions: Sanskrit kavya (for example, in the metaphor-laden description of female beauty — 'charm as that of the land-lotus half-scorched and half radiant by the noon-day'), or the Gothic novel (in the evocation of terror: dark dungeons lit by 'a solitary and feeble lamp' while 'massive doors creaked on their hinges'). *Rajmohan's Wife* prefigures some of the concerns that surface later in Bankim's Bangla novels where he returns to realism and to contemporary life — the stealing of a will (*Krishnakanter Will*, 1876), extra-marital passion (*Visha-briksha*, 1873) female initiative (*Indira*, 1873), childhood attachment growing into adolescent love (*Chandrashekhar*, 1875), and several other less worked out motifs. Yet this novel has never been read and remembered as these others have been. The different receptions accorded to Bankim's English novel and his novels in Bangla raise several interlinked questions. Was *Rajmohan's Wife* a false start because the author chose to write in English, or was it because it deployed a narrative model which, for whatever reason, turned out to be unsuitable for his purpose at that moment? Does choice of language — hence inescapably of audience — inadvertently condition the semantic connotations of a text or implicitly determine its ideological base?[5] As the novel was being serialized, was the writer himself affected by the awareness of the lack of a sizeable reading community, a suspicion that gets confirmed by the author's declining involvement in the events of the novel in the later chapters and an undue sense of haste at the end? In literary discourse causes and effects can never be conclusively established but questions like these will be further explored in the brief analysis of the novel that is attempted here.

IV

The elaborate unfolding of the plot and the intricate relationships among the dramatis personae create the impression that *Raj-mohan's Wife* was intended to be a longer novel than it actually turned out to be. The dyadic introduction of the characters in the first two chapters (two women in one and two men in the other, with sharply contrasting attributes and sartorial details in each case), and the depiction of Matangini's misery in the third, is followed by a long and complicated genealogical flashback whose purpose might have been to provide hereditary or environmental justification for the behaviour patterns of the characters. Mathur and Madhav are collaterals descended from a scheming ancestor who appropriated money through dubious means to rise in society. Though the author does not state this explicitly, Mathur's crudity may be attributed to his half-baked village education (we are told his father condemned an English school 'as a thing not only useless, but positively mischievous'), while Madhav's refinement may be the result of the English education he received in Calcutta. Madhav's father was actually attracted to the city by the luxury and profligacy Calcutta promised to young men with money, but the unexpected by-product of this move was the exposure of his son to the new liberal humanist ethos of English education. The dialogic myth of Calcutta that was to evolve through the nineteenth century (the city as a site for culture and refinement as well as for debauchery and moral degradation) is already quite visible here, as for example in the conversation between Mathur and Madhav in chapter 2 and later in the women's talk about rural and urban hair styles in chapter 14.

In many of Bankimchandra's Bangla novels the English-knowing urban dilettante is the butt of author's ridicule (for example, Debendra in *Krishnakanter Will*), but in *Rajmohan's Wife* Madhav's knowledge of English and his Calcutta background are set up as signs of moral superiority over Mathur who stares at the women as they return from the river carrying water, indulges in bawdy gossip and uses illegal means to satisfy his craving for money. At a crucial moment in the narrative we find Madhav Ghose reclining on a 'mahogany couch covered with satin. A single but well-fed light illumined the chamber. Some two or three English books were scattered over the couch and one of them Madhav held in his hand ... ' The English books are obviously signifiers of a more civilized way of life — as is the western furniture — to which Mathur Ghose, despite his money, power and 'mofussil magnificence' can never aspire. In Mathur's bedchamber the varnish of the almirahs and chests has been 'considerably ... soiled by time and rough usage' and the walls are decorated with two large paintings 'from one of which glowered the grim black figure of Kali and the other ... displayed the crab-like form of Durga'. The unusually negative charge in the description of the goddesses is surprising because in Bankim's Bangla writing we never find these icons treated in such a dismissive manner. These instances make one return to the question posited earlier — how much does the choice of the writer's language (hence of audience) determine his tone and attitude?

While in most of Bankimchandra's Bangla novels the Englishman is either the abductor or the adversary (see p. 16), in *Rajmohan's Wife* the white man is ascribed a positive and stabilizing function. When the seemingly invincible local alliance of patriarchy, criminality and money more or less destroys Matangini by the end of the novel, the only redressal, almost as divine retribution, comes from the fair-minded white administrator — a shrewd and restlessly active Irishman. This unquestioning faith in colonial justice surfaces only very intermittently in nineteenth-century Bangla fiction — as, for example, in Rabindranath Tagore's short story 'Didi' — deftly analysed by Gayatri Chakrborty Spivak,[6] but more often than not British rule is perceived as oppressive and exploitative. Certainly nowhere in Bankimchandra's Bangla corpus do we find the justice and efficiency of imperial rule so unequivocally, if briefly, proclaimed as in his solitary English novel, *Rajmohan's Wife*.

The criminals are duly punished at the end of the novel, but even the British legal system is powerless to redeem Matangini. When in the last chapter just desserts are meted out to all the characters according to the conventions of British Victorian novels, Matangini poses a problem for the author. She cannot be returned to the conjugal space from which she has dislodged herself through an emotionally sanctioned but socially unforgivable act. Sending her back to her parents' home is a temporary solution, after which an early death becomes expedient for the tidiness of the closure as well as the resolution of the author's own moral dilemma. By making her confess her love for a person not her husband, the author pushes Matangini into an uncharted and ambiguous territory from which neither romantic sympathy nor colonial justice can deliver her to a positive future. The object of her love, Madhav, has been refined by his English education into such a paragon of scrupulous virtue that, when Matangini confronts him with her passion, all he can do is to weep and implore her to forget him. Matangini is impetuous and brave, but the author weighs down her confession with a rhetoric of guilt ('sinful', 'impure felicity', 'you cannot hate me more than I hate myself', etc.) so that she already stands condemned. Whatever may have been the author's moral design, despite his correctness of conduct, the passive and indecisive Madhav gets quite overshadowed in this text by the fiery heroine.

Matangini is the first in a series of strong and transgressive women in Bankimchandra's novels (Ayesha in *Durgeshnandini*, Rohini in *Krishnakanter Will*, Shaibalini in *Chandrashekhar* are some of the others), who have to be relentlessly punished even though the author and the reader may understand and admire their rebellion. Women's agency is foregrounded, but with a simultaneous reminder of the disruptive social potential of its assertive aspect. Characterization is not Bankim's forte in this apprentice novel. Matangini only occasionally gets illuminated as a character. The other characters remain sketchy by and large, but what really disturbs the reader is the abruptness of the end: 'As to Madhav, Champak and the rest, some are dead and the others will die. Throwing this flood of light on their past and future history, I bid you, good reader, "FAREWELL".'

This breezy assertion of universal mortality in retrospect makes all story-telling redundant. But such an ending could have been the author's way of getting out of a serialization project that was no longer engaging his interest.

V

The suffering of women is central to *Rajmohan's Wife* and it tended to be one of the major concerns in Indian fiction for several decades to come. Not only do half of Bankimchandra's novels have women as protagonists, but many of his contemporary novelists in Bengal and other parts of India also focused on women and their predicament. From the first Marathi novel *Yamuna Paryatan* (1857), to its late nineteenth-century successor *Pan Lakshyant Kon Gheto* (1890), from the early Hindi novel *Devrani Jethani ki Kahani* (1870) to Premchand's *Nirmala* (1926), the examples can be multiplied from almost any Indian language.[7]

It is not entirely a coincidence that several major European novels of the nineteenth century also have women as their protagonists (e.g. *Emma, Vanity Fair, Jane Eyre, Madame Bovary, Anna Karen-ina, Middlemarch, Portrait of a Lady, Tess of the Durbervilles*). Classic realism, which was the dominant fictional mode of the time, attempted to convey in concrete and specific details the complex relationship between individuals and the society by whose code they were expected to live. The resultant tension could be studied in sharper contours when the protagonist's life was restricted within a narrow space with very few options regarding mobility, economic self-sufficiency or vocation — in other words, when the protagonist was a woman. In most cultures, social conformity has always been more obligatory for a woman than for a man, her identity generally constructed — by herself as much as by others — in terms of her relationship with men, as daughter, wife, mother or widow. Although in the present novel Rajmohan interests us very little as a person, Matangini's identity, as announced in the title, is irrevocably connected to her marital status.

Apart from this beautiful and spirited woman wasted on a brutal and surly husband, there are other female characters in the novel — Kanak, married to an absent and polygamous husband who, according to the custom of Kulin Brahmans, is not obliged to provide her with a home, and Tara, the wife of a powerful landlord, superseded in her husband's affection by a younger and prettier wife — providing three variations on the theme of wifely misery. Compared to some of the magnificent later heroines of Bankim-chandra's Bangla novels — Kapalkundala, Prafulla or Shanti — these women seem somewhat perfunctorily sketched, but they certainly engage our attention more than the men in this novel who are either meekly virtuous or melodramatically villainous. The scenes around the women, specially the vivid descriptions of group activities in the interiors of the houses, contribute to the reading pleasure of the novel, evoking an ethos that is vibrant with life. Two chapters stand out. The mock-serious account of the bustle and commotion in the kitchen courtyard in chapter 5 where cooks, servant women, children and girls with tinkling ankle-bells vie with each other to keep the decibel level permanently high; and a more relaxed scene in chapter 14, when the slanting rays of the later afternoon sun fall at regular intervals through the balcony rails in an upstairs veranda where women sit around dressing each others' hair or painting their feet with 'red lac', discussing the different ways of braiding hair in Radhaganj and Calcutta, reiterating a recurring concern of the novelist — the relative merits of rural East Bengal and the urbanized West Bengal dominated by Calcutta. But both these engaging scenes are suddenly shattered by the unexpected arrivals of the masters of the houses, abruptly silencing the women into awe and making them scurry and hide from the authoritarian male gaze. In positions of absolute power, the masters of the house, depending on their mood, can order instant obedience, punish defiance or confer favour. Compared to this predictable man–woman relationship, the equations among the women across the classes have a more nuanced texture in the novel — of mutual bonding, subtle rivalry, friendship, sympathy or betrayal. Suki's mother and Karuna, domestic servants both, become, within the limited frame of this brief novel, as concretely realized as the landlord's wives.

The mood of the novel changes very fast and frequently within the span of its 126 pages. Domestic disharmony, legal intrigue, criminal conspiracy, passionate but forbidden love and dark incarceration in dungeons alternate in rapid succession. One of the most memorable of its many shifting scenes is Matangini's solitary journey in the dark night through forest, water, storm and lightning, redolent with literary echoes of Radha's tryst with Krishna in Vaishnava poetry, when she braved the elements to meet Krishna secretly. Where Matangini lets her long hair loose in the water of the pond around her fair face to avoid detection in the moonlight, in this rootedness in a recognizable literary culture we catch a glimpse of what Bankim would be able to achieve when he would no longer be inhibited by the anxiety of tailoring his sensibility to suit the cloth of English idioms and metaphors.

VI

Bankimchandra's English novel was quite evidently hampered by the absence of the range of registers available to him in his Bangla writing — from the sonorous Sanskrit or heavily Persianized diction to the earthy raciness of Prakrit and the vitality of local dialects. In English he had by and large one linguistic code at his disposal — the formal literary style to which his class of men had been exposed through two generations of English education. Bankimchandra Chatterjee was one of seven students in the first graduating batch when the University of Calcutta was set up. Before he went up to Hoogly College he had already studied English from two Englishmen Stydd and Sinclair in Midnapore School. While studying English in college he started publishing poetry in Bangla journals like *Sambad Prabhakar* and *Sambad Sudhiranjan*, but he chose English for his first sustained piece of prose — which was written six years after he came out of college. Bangla did not have a model of novel writing at that time — he was obviously emulating examples from English literature — but the tradition of poetry was long and alive in Bengal. As it turned out in the long run, however, neither poetry in Bangla nor fiction in English was going to be his true vocation.

After joining government service as a Deputy Magistrate Bankim appears to have stopped writing in Bangla for a few years. His first attempt at writing after he begun his official career seems to have been made at the request of Kishori Chand Mitra, who might have been Bankim's colleague in the Bengal Civil Service had he not been dismissed around the time that Bankim had his first posting in Khulna. It seems curious that the dismissed civil servant, an active member of various social reform organizations and the brother of Pearey Chand Mitra — who is remembered as the author of the first novel in Bangla — should decide to start a journal in English, and not in Bangla. It is in this short-lived and small-circulation journal *Indian Field* that *Rajmohan's Wife* was serialized in 1864.

'English education' by this time had begun to assume a unique role in the lives of the Calcutta elite, as also in the lives of the elite in other metropolitan areas of India. The University of Bombay was started in 1858 along with the universities of Calcutta and Madras, and in 1882 Krishna Vishnu Chiplunkar wrote 'Crushed by English poetry ... Our freedom was destroyed',[8] using poetry in a moment of creative clarity as a synecdoche for the entire range of Western influences. Yet at the same time English poetry was also perceived as a liberating agent rather than an enslaving force. Rabindranath Tagore wrote about his responses to Shakespeare and Shelley: 'our hearts naturally craved the life-bringing shock of the passionate emotions expressed in English literature. Ours was not the aesthetic enjoyment of literary art, but the jubilant welcome of a turbulent wave from a situation of stagnation ... '[9]

This ambivalence towards English literature and what it stood for continued through the nineteenth century, and possibly also later. Meanwhile, the word 'education' had come to be synonymous with English education, of which the study of English literature comprised a major part. In the words of Nirad C. Chaudhuri:

From the second quarter of the nineteenth century the word education which had passed into Bengali speech, sometimes in the contracted form of "ejoo", was applied only to those who knew English well, as never to anyone else, however learned they may be in Sanskrit or Bengali. A profound scholar who might have been a great authority on Vedanta philosophy, would have been called a Pundit, but never an educated man.[10]

This had behavioural implications among urban Bengali males

(with a few notable exceptions, women in the nineteenth century were not part of the charmed circle of the 'educated') even outside literary and intellectual domains. It is sometimes assumed that while English was becoming the language of formal and public discourse, Bangla remained the language of intimacy and personal relationships. But there is enough evidence from the nineteenth century to indicate that frequently English was the language of informal correspondence as well, if not of conversation, when both parties happened to know English. Michael Madhusudan Dutt, long after his dramatic abandonment of English as his language of creative expression, continued to write letters to his friends in English about his personal concerns. [11] In another part of India we have the example of Govardhanram Tripathi who kept a detailed personal diary in English to record the many unresolved conflicts of his life, while he earned fame and eminence by writing the massive four-volume novel *Saraswatichandra* (1887–1900) in Gujarati.

Letters between fathers and sons tended to be in English when both were 'educated', and Nirad C. Chaudhuri with his unerring eye for cultural incongruities observes how Bangla almanacs, normally consulted for astrological information necessary for regulating daily life, came by the end of the century also to include model letters in English for the use of fathers and sons. As an example of how language can transform modes of thought and behaviour, he cites one such letter where, in response to a request for more money from the son studying in Calcutta, the father writes: 'Your mother, like myself, feels grieved' at such extravagance. Chaudhuri comments:

No Hindu father would refer to the mother in discussing money matters with his son and if he did, it would be "I and your mother" rather than "your mother and I" which the language necessitates. We could not write in English without changing mentally. We could not merely pay the tithe of mint and anise and cumin to the language and omit the weightier matter of revising our attitudes towards our wives and husbands. [12]

It may not be easy to determine how much of this revision was merely a matter of surface adjustments to temporarily accommodate the demands of English phraseology, and how much actually percolated to the level of perception or consciousness. This question occasionally surfaces while we read *Rajmohan's Wife*. When an unsophisticated village woman of East Bengal is made to exclaim 'Go to Jericho!' as a phrase of friendly remonstrance, or when the author chooses certain lexical items external to the ethos of the story (e.g. 'olive' to describe a woman's complexion, or 'Billingsgate' to describe low or vituperative language) the reader is troubled by the thought that a second hand and bookish predilection is regulating expression. A more serious question about the compatibility between culture and language arises when Matangini is made to articulate her illicit love for her brother-in-law in the passionate language of English Romantic poetry.

After *Rajmohan's Wife*, Bankim never attempted to write imaginative literature in English, though he continued to write essays and discursive pieces in English and actively participated in various debates about religion and culture in the columns of local English newspapers. He was the second major example in nineteenth-century Bengal of a writer making such an abrupt shift of linguistic gear. Michael Madhusudan Dutt, fourteen years older than Bankim and a student of Henry Derozio, had always dreamt of being an English poet. He wrote *The Captive Ladie* (1849) and *Visions of the Past* (1848) in English and, in an imagined fellowship with the great poets of England, dedicated one of his poems to Wordsworth. In a letter to his friend Gaurdas Basak he wrote in English:

I am reading Tom Moore's life of my favourite Byron — splendid book upon my word! Oh! How I should like to see you writing my life, if I happen to be a great poet — which I am almost sure I shall be if I go to England.[13]

He did go to England later; yet eventually he came to be remembered not as a poet in English but as the most important poet in

Bangla in the nineteenth century who energized the language, introduced new poetic forms, and drew upon the resources of the *Ramayana* and *Mahabharata* as well as Milton and Virgil to revitalize its rhetoric. There was no visible opposition in his case between the decision to write in Bangla and the admiration for western literary practices. One of his Bangla sonnets pays homage to 'Fanscisco Petrarcha, the poet of Italy' who gave him a gem to dedicate to Saraswati 'which the goddess was pleased to accept'. This easy give-and-take between the muses of different civilizations was made possible through Dutt's familiarity with not only English and Bangla but also other European languages. A much-quoted Bangla sonnet written when Dutt was living in penury at Versailles dramatizes the moment when he realized the folly of writing in a borrowed language. The sonnet dwells on the humiliation of begging at alien doors while the treasure-chest of his mother tongue lay unopened.[14]

Bankimchandra never made any such literary statement either about his decision to write in English or about his return to his mother tongue. If he did so in personal correspondence or conversation, these have not survived. Even after he abandoned English as a medium for imaginative literature, he remained alert to the political possibilities of English as the language of national consolidation. In the first issue of *Bangadarshan*, the journal that he founded in 1872, he wrote: 'There are certain issues that do not pertain to the Bengalis alone, where the whole of India has to be addressed. Unless we use English for such discourse, how will the rest of the country understand?'[15] But elsewhere we also find him exhorting creative writers not to write only for the educated few (which writing in English evidently implied) and to address a wider range of readers. If the use of English had a distinctly elite bias that excluded the lower class, lower castes, and rural people, it also left out the women who might have belonged to the author's own family. In a remarkable satiric sketch Bankim makes fun of the English-knowing Bengali babu who is contemptuous of books in his mother tongue, taking pride in his familiarity with English literature. In contrast, his wife emerges as a more authentic and integrated person, who — uncontaminated by the enslaving language — enjoys Bangla fiction enthusiastically and without embarrassment. Bankim reminded his fellow-writers in Bengal of this large and vital readership.

By the 1870s Bankimchandra was convinced that English was the language of polemics in India, but not of creative literature. It is well-known that he admonished Romesh Chandra Dutt, a member of the heaven-born Indian Civil Service and the future author of *The Economic History of India*, for not writing in his mother tongue. In the highly westernized Dutt family to which Romesh Chandra belonged, as did his celebrated poet-cousins Toru and Oru, Bangla had never been considered a language worthy of cultivation, and he confessed a lack of formal knowledge of the language. Bankim dismissed this reason for not writing in his mother tongue, insisting that whatever educated young men like him wrote would become the standard language. He said:

You will never live by your writing in English ... Look at others, Your uncles Govind Chandra and Sashi Chandra and Madhusudan Dutt were the best educated men of Hindu College in their day. Govind Chandra and Sashi Chandra's English poems will never live, Madhusudan's Bengali poetry will live as long as the Bengali language will live.[16]

These words must have created an impression on the young I.C.S. officer, because two years later Romesh Chandra wrote his first novel *Banga-Bijeta* in 1874, and went on to write five more that have secured him a permanent place in the history of the Bangla novel.

Bankim's advice to Romesh Chandra Dutt was prophetic indeed. Except for the researcher in nineteenth-century Indian-English poetry, no one now knows the names of Sashi Chandra or Govind Chandra Dutt (they spelt their names in English as

Soshee Chunder and Govin Chunder), nor would we know the name of Bankimchandra Chatterjee if he had stopped after writing *Rajmohan's Wife*. Bankim's contemporaries may or may not have paid much attention to this novel. But reading it today after a gap of a century and three decades, with the advantages of hindsight, we see this text as a potent site for discussing crucial issues about language, culture, colonization and representation.

Notes

1. Some of them are: Sisir Kumar Das (*The Artist in Chains: The Life of Bankimchandra Chatterjee*, New Delhi, 1984); Tapan Raychaudhuri (*Europe Reconsidered; Perceptions of the West in Nineteenth-Century Bengal*, Delhi, 1988); Jasodhara Bagchi ('Positivism and Nationalism: Womanhood and Crisis in Nationalist Fiction: Bankimchandra's *Anandamath*', in *Narrative: Forms and Transformations*, Sudhakar Marathe and Meenakshi Mukherjee, eds, Delhi, 1986); Sabyasachi Bhattacharya (in *Bankimchandra: Essays in Perspective*, ed. Bhabatosh Chatterjee, Calcutta: Sahitya Akademi, 1994); Ranajit Guha (*An Indian Historiography of India: A Nineteenth Century Agenda*, Calcutta, 1985); Tanika Sarkar ('Bankimchandra and the Impossibility of a Political Agenda', New Delhi; Occasional Papers Series of NMML, 1991); Partha Chatterjee (*Nationalist Thought and the Colonial World*, New Delhi, 1986); and Sudipta Kaviraj (*The Unhappy Consciousness: Bankimchandra Chattopadhyay and the Formation of Nationalist Discourse in India*, Delhi, 1995).

2. Nirad C. Chaudhuri wrote:

> The two men who created modern Bengali literature wrote their first works in English before they even thought of writing anything in Bengali. The creator of modern Bengali poetry wrote his first long poem in English, and the creator of Bengali fiction his first novel. But both of them found that to do so was to go into a blind alley which led nowhere. For this reason they turned to Bengali ...

('Opening Address', *The Eye of the Beholder*, Maggie Butcher (ed.), London, 1983).

Sisir Kumar Das wrote:

> [*Rajmohan's Wife*] was little known outside an intimate circle and was soon forgotten ... Bankim thought of translating this into Bengali and in fact he

did translate the first nine chapters. He did not complete the job perhaps because he thought it was too unsatisfactory to receive any public attention.

The Artist in Chains: The Life of Bankimchandra Chatterjee, New Delhi, 1984, p. 190.

Jogesh Chandra Bagal wrote: 'Bankim's literary temperament could not be satisfied with writing fiction in English and ... he began writing *Durgesh-nandini*' (my translation). (*Bankim Rachanabali*, vol. I, Calcutta: Sahitya Samsad, first pub. 1955, present edn. 1980, p. xiv.)

3. Bankim Chandra Chatterjee by a Bengali, *Induprakash*, 16 July to 27 August 1894. These articles were signed 'Zero'. The present quotation is from the fifth article, 'His Literary History', reprinted in *The Harmony of Virtue*, p. 90.

4. Two very characteristic statements included in this volume, *Bankim-chandra: Essays in Perspective* (ed. Bhabatosh Chatterjee, Calcutta: Sahitya Akademi, 1994), are quoted below:

> Bankim started his literary journey with *Rajmohan's Wife* written in English, but his real achievement began with *Durgeshnandini*
>
> (Saroj Bandopadhyay, p. 449).

> *Rajmohan's Wife* shows no sign of genius, nor did it arouse much interest among the readers when it was being serialized. This literary effort by India's first Bachelor of Arts — Bankimchandra — was in the same mould as all the other poems, stories and essays that used to be written in those days by those who had newly been educated in English
>
> (Sunil Gangopadhyay, p. 390).

There is, however, one critic in this volume who does not dismiss this novel, but her claim that the novel had 'immediate readership' all over India is not substantiated by evidence: 'Because it [*Rajmohan's Wife*] transcended the linguistic barrier, the novel gained immediate readership from Indians who belonged to states other than Bengal' (Prema Nandakumar, p. 400).

The tendency to claim Bankimchandra as an originary figure of the Indian novel in English is a very recent one. Ganeshwar Mishra elsewhere writes: '[Bankim] considerably influenced the Indo-Anglian and Indian language writers of the late nineteenth and early twentieth century' ('The Indian Narrative Tradition and Bankim Chandra's *Rajmohan's Wife*', *Journal of Literary Studies*, vol. 4, no. I, p. 59). While Bankim's Bangla novels certainly influenced Indian-language writers — not only in Bangla — but, through a chain of translations, some writers in Hindi, Marathi and Kannada as well, the claim that he influenced Indian writers in English would be very hard to sustain, even though he may be the unwitting founder of a genre that now has high visibility.

5. For a detailed description of the emergence of the novel in Indian languages, see chapters I and II of Meenakshi Muherjee, *Realism and Reality: The Novel and Society in India* (Delhi: Oxford University Press, 1985).

6. See 'The Burden of English Studies', Gayatri Chakraborty Spivak in *The Lie of the Land: English Literary Studies in India*, ed. Rajeshwari Sunder Rajan (Delhi: Oxford University Press, 1992).

7. See chapter IV, 'Women in a New Genre', in *Realism and Reality*.

8. Quoted by Sudhir Chandra in *The Oppressive Present: Literature and Social Consciousness in Colonial India* (Delhi: Oxford University Press, 1992).

9. From the English translation of Rabindranath Tagore's *Jibansmriti* (Bangla, 1912) published in English as *My Reminiscences* (New York, 1914), p. 181.

10. 'Opening Address' by Nirad C. Chaudhuri in *The Eye of the Beholder*, ed. Maggie Butcher (London, 1983), p. 11.

11. See Introduction in *Madhusudan Rachanabali*, ed. Kshetra Gupta (Calcutta: Sahitya Samsad, 1965).

12. Nirad C. Chaudhuri in *The Eye of the Beholder*, p. 10

13. See p. xii, *Madhusudan Rachanabali*.

14. Sonnet 3 in 'Chaturdashpadi Kavitavali', p. 159, *Madhusudan Rachanabali*. For a prose paraphrase of the sonnet see p. 23.

15. Quoted by the editor, Jogesh Chandra Bagal, *Bankim Rachanabali*, vol. I (Calcutta: Sahitya Samsad, 1955), p. xvi.

16. Ibid., p. xxvii.

3

Churning the Seas of Treacle: Three Ways

Although the 1930s are generally seen as the take-off decade for the Indian novel in English, its genealogy can be traced quite far back into the previous century. These early novels appeared at a time when the genre was in an initial and tentative stage in the country and, before the new paradigms got indigenized, different varieties of pre-novel narratives appeared in print in many Indian languages.[1] Even in English — at that time hardly a language of literary activity in India — a couple of unusual short narratives from journals have been unearthed, which could be seen as the earliest attempts at writing fiction in the newly introduced language.[2] Curiously, neither of them shares the ideological and other presuppositions of the English novels that were to follow in the subsequent decades in India. After a glance at these two short narratives, this essay will concentrate on three representative early novels in English, to examine the heterogeneity as well as certain common concerns of these writers in English and to situate them in the larger map of multi-lingual India. *Govinda Samanta* or *The History of a Bengali Raiyat* (1874) by Lal Behari Day is a saga of subaltern life, probably the first fictional attempt in any Indian language to deal with people below the middle class; *Sanjogita* or *The Princess of Aryavarta* (1902) by K.K. Sinha, written at a time when historical romances were popular in Bangla, Hindi, Urdu and Marathi as well, retells the popular Prithviraj–Sanjogita story, which offered a blueprint for the projection of a heroic Hindu masculinity and the ideal of a *veerangana* who would nevertheless remain a paragon of wifely virtue; and lastly, *Prince of Destiny: The New Krishna* (1909) by Sarath Kumar Ghosh, a philosophical reflection on the moral and cultural transactions between two civilizations. *Prince of Destiny*, a 629-page novel of epic proportions, first published in England and later reprinted in the Colonial Edition ('For circulation in the British Colonies and India only'), is located in the princely state of 'Barathpur', evidently an allegory for India. Mimetic, heroic and ruminative respectively, the narrative modes of the three novels traverse a wide spectrum, anticipating a few of the directions English novels were destined to take in India.

II

The earliest extant narrative texts in India may well be two tracts of imaginary history written by Kylas Chunder Dutt and Soshee Chunder Dutt in 1835 and 1845 respectively. Both 'A Journal of Forty Eight Hours of the Year 1945' by Kylas Chunder and Soshee Chunder's 'The Republic of Orissa: A Page from the Annals of the 20th Century' project into the future to describe battles of liberation against the British, anticipating events which they expected would happen in the next century; but the two pieces end with dissimilar resolutions. Both are works of very young men: Kylas Chunder Dutt is described as 'A Student of Hindu College' in *The Calcutta Literary Gazette* (6 June 1835) where his piece appeared and he seemed eager to display newly-acquired scholarship by using a fiery passage on liberty from *Junius Brutus* as an epigraph.[3] Soshee Chunder was twenty-one when he wrote his rebellious piece in *The Saturday Evening Harakuru* (25 May 1845). We know from his subsequent writing that maturity and experience would considerably temper his radicalism in later years.

Kylas Chunder Dutt fixed on a year more than a century after the time of composition as the crucial moment when India would make a bid to gain freedom (as it happens he was only two years off the mark) by which time, he felt, the people of India would have reached their limits of tolerance. His piece begins thus:

The people of India and particularly those of the metropolis had been subject for the last fifty years to every species of subaltern oppression. The dagger and the bowl were dealt out with a merciless hand, and neither age, sex, nor condition could repress the rage of the British barbarians. Those events, together with the recollection of the grievances suffered by their ancestors roused the dormant spirit of the generally considered timid Indians.

This is followed by a detailed description of the battles between the British, led by the Governor Lord Fell Butcher and Colonel John Blood-thirsty, and a large Indian army of patriots who took their orders from Bhoobun Mohan, a charismatic young graduate possessing 'all the learning and eloquence which the Anglo-Indian college could furnish'. In the first round the patriots were victorious, but perhaps the compulsions of his own colonized circumstances made the author desist from pushing this euphoric state too far. A much more accomplished writer had to face a similar predicament nearly fifty years later when in *Anandamath* (1882) the victory of the *santans* against the combined forces of the foreign rulers had to be renegotiated to fit in with contemporary history. In Kylas Chunder Dutt's account the Indians got routed badly in their attempt to capture the Fort William in Calcutta and Bhoobun Mohan was sentenced to death. As he uttered his last words of exhortation to his companions to carry on his struggle, his head was 'severed from his body at a single blow'.

The second text 'The Republic of Orissa' (1845), coming ten years later, was even more unusual in that the resistance against the British here was led not by an English-educated urban youth, but by a tribal from Orissa, the intrepid Bheekoo Barik, the chief of the Kingaries. This early interest in a tribal hero anticipates Soshee Chunder Dutt's subsequent scholarly preoccupation with tribal life and history as evident in the last volume of his six-volume collected Works, titled *The Wild Tribes of India*.[4] The immediate provocation for the battle was the passing of an imaginary 'Slavery Act' by the British in 1916 which was for Dutt a remote date seventy-one years away in the future. The rebelling forces from Bengal, Bihar and Orissa combined to defeat an army of ten thousand Irish soldiers commanded by Sir J. Proudfoot and capture the fort of Radanaugger. Their victory forced the British to offer some concessions, which they 'deceitfully deferred fulfilling' when the immediate danger was over. The military strand in the narrative is woven in and reinforced by a love story, through which the smouldering fire of the Kingaries is rekindled after five years to cause another confrontation with the British in 1921. 'On the 13th January of the following year, Orissa proclaimed its independence and though the government of Pillibheet [the fictitious capital of British India] refused to recognize it, their armies completely evacuated that province, after a few vain efforts to disturb its independence.' Even though Dutt does not claim that the whole country was freed from British rule at that point, the general thrust at the end suggests the gradual decline of the empire after that:

We regret its fallen grandeur, we regret to see an imperial bird, shorn of its wings and plumage of pride, coming down precipitately from its airy height.

The wishful and exuberant imagination displayed in these two tracts not only proclaim the extreme youth and ardour of the writers, they also tell us of the relative openness of the English press in India which published these pieces advocating armed insurgency against the British. Censorship was to grow more stringent as the century progressed, beginning with the passing of power from the East India Company to the Crown. By the last quarter of the nineteenth century historical novels became very popular in several major Indian languages, and to a limited extent in English as well, as a vehicle of emerging nationalism because patriotism could be expressed only when couched in stories of the pre-British past. Flashing forward to the future to challenge the present rule, as the young Dutts did, was not a literary act likely to be repeated.

III

These early tracts, though written by college-educated young men, both from the highly-westernized Dutt family of Rambagan (Calcutta) that produced a number of minor poets in English in the nineteenth century are surprisingly free from the overt dependence on canonical literary texts from England, echoes of which would permeate most of the longer narratives in English that follow; nor do they seem weighed down by the burden of servility that the English language indirectly conferred on most of the novelists. It has been argued in the previous chapters that very few Indian writers in English dared to be critical of the British in the nineteenth century or in the decades immediately following it, and any expression of national pride was carefully removed in time to glorify ancient India before the Sultanate and Mughal regimes. It is fairly common to find in the novels of this period paeans of praise for the exemplary role of the British in rescuing the country from the 'anarchy and despotism' of the Muslim rulers. ('Undoubtedly, the British government is the sun of our system: if it were taken away, our entire fabric would fall to pieces', *Sanjogita*, p. 267.) Apart from political acquiescence, their cultural subjugation too was demonstrated in the frequent and proud display of their familiarity with English literature. Gratuitous quotations and unnecessary allusions to western texts punctuated their books and their narratives were dotted with authorial intrusions directed at 'the gentle reader', as was the practice of some of their Victorian models.

Even *Govinda Samanta* (1874), a stark and moving account of a Bengali peasant's life, is not free of these trappings. One is surprised at the discrepancy between its slavish external markers attempting to establish the right literary pedigree, and a smouldering anger at the exploitation of the rural poor that exists as a subtext. It is probably the earliest novel in any Indian language to describe the life of this oppressed class of people, although in drama Dinabandhu Mitra had already initiated a tradition of protest plays in Bangla with his *Neel Darpan* (1860) — which were followed by *Jamidar Darpan* by Mir Musarraf Hussain and *Chakar Darpan* by Dakshina Charan Chattopadhyay. All these dealt with oppression of the poor — by indigo planters, landlords and tea planters. It is surprising therefore that *Govinda Samanta*, which seems to belong to this tradition, should begin with an unashamed replication of the famous 'bill of fare' metaphor with which Henry Fielding opens the first chapter of *Tom Jones* (1748):

I therefore ... propose to tell you at once, in all sincerity and good faith, what you are to expect and what not to expect in this hall of refreshment; so that after being acquainted with the bill of fare, you may either begin to partake of the repast or not, just as you please. (*Govinda Samanta*, p. 1)

The novel abounds in many such external indicators that the author is well-versed in the conventions of novel-writing in England — and these include an avowal of realism through the declared rejection of the non-realist ingredients found in the stories of older Indian writers:

You are not to expect anything marvellous or wonderful in this little book. My great Indian predecessors ... have treated of kings with ten heads and twenty arms; of a monkey carrying the sun in his arm-pit ... of being man above and fish below, or with the body of a man and the head of an elephant. (p. 2)

The vehemence of Lal Behari Day's rejection of traditional modes of story-telling almost matches Macaulay's contempt for what passed for knowledge in India: 'History, abounding with kings thirty feet high and reigns thirty thousand years long and Geography made up of seas of treacle and seas of butter.'[5] This Utilitarian impatience with mythic imagination and the dismissal of traditional iconography played a major role in evolving the course of Indian art and literature in the late nineteenth century. Macaulay's echo can be heard in O. Chandu Menon's well-known manifesto on realism in the introductory pages of his Malayalam novel *Indulekha* (1889):

Before the European style of oil painting began to be known and appreciated in this country, we had painted, in defiance of all possible existence, pictures of Vishnu as half man and half lion ... pictures of god Krishna with his legs twisted and turned into positions in which no biped could stand ... [6]

Menon welcomed the new taste in painting that 'delineated men, beasts and things according to their true appearance' and stories 'composed of incidents true to natural life'. Day is not alone among his contemporaries in rejecting the 'sea of treacle' and thirty-feet-high kings, but what strikes us is the openly imitative manner in which he wrote his introduction when the body of his novel is far from imitative. His slavish framing of the novel does not prepare the reader for the elemental force of the core narrative that traces the declining fortunes of a poor peasant family of the Ugrakshatriya caste, living in the Bardhaman district of what is now West Bengal. The family is by the end of the novel rendered destitute and landless through the vagaries of climate, disease, oppressions of the landlord and stifling demands of the community. A sub-plot depicting the torture of the indigo planters that affects another branch of the family bravely links the novel with *Neel Darpan*, a

play which had incurred official displeasure. The English translation of Dinabandhu Mitra's play had already been banned and
its publisher Reverend James Long jailed. Soon after *Govinda
Samanta* was published the infamous Dramatic Performance Control Act (1876) put a curb on the expression of any discontent with
British presence on stage. It is against this background that Lal
Behari Day's novel has to be read.

Initially begun as an entry to a contest announced by a Bengali
zamindar to document rural life, *Govinda Samanta* soon transcends the parameters of ethnography. It spans the seasonal and
life-cycle of the Samanta family from 1820 — the year in which
the last Sati was performed in the region — to 1870, the year of
the great famine. It starts as the account of a stable and seemingly
'organic' community, whose life is structured as it were by a
predictable rhythm, to establish which Day describes planting,
harvests, sugar-cane crushing, feasts and festivals to mark birth,
death and marriage, illness and healing methods, games, storytel-
ling and other routine activities of the village. There are moments
of humour and banter as when describing and classifying local
ghosts according to religion, caste and gender — because they are
very much part of the village community. He comments light-
heartedly on the difficulty of rendering the speech of these ghosts
in English spelling because 'Bengali ghosts speak strongly through
their nose'. (p. 75) But gradually the mood darkens as the noose
tightens around Govinda Samanta's neck. An epidemic is followed
by famine, resulting in debt, loss of land, and migration to the city
where he becomes a nameless daily-wage labour. The novel ends
with Govinda's ignominious death there. When the manuscript
was submitted for the contest these later chapters which lift the
novel above its documentary status had not been written. In its
totality it is a devastating document. Nothing like this existed in
Indian fiction at that time. Fakir Mohan Senapati's Oriya novel
about how a landlord's greed turns a peasant into a destitute, *Chha*

Mana Atha Guntha, written powerfully with a grim humour, was serialized in *Utkal Sahitya* at the end of the century and published as a book in 1902. *Govinda Samanta* might even be seen as precursor to the Hindi classic *Godan* (1936), though Premchand may never have known about the existence of this book. It seems surprising today that the first subaltern novel in India should have been written in English.

IV

At the turn of the century when K.K. Sinha wrote his second novel *Sanjogita, or The Princess of Aryavarta* (1903) historical novels were the rage in India. Rajput history was a common quarry for Hindi, Bangla and Marathi novelists, and the story of Prithviraj and Sanjogita was one of the favourites. Ganga Prasad Gupta wrote *Veerpatni or Rani Sanjogita* (Hindi) in the same year that Sinha's novel was published in English, and Baldev Prasad Misra's novel *Prithviraj Chauhan* (also Hindi) had come out the previous year. Such repetitions were not unusual because the sources and the impulses were often the same. From the seed of one particular paragraph in James Tod's *Annals and Antiquities of Rajasthan* (1829) at least three well-known novels had sprouted: *Rajsingha* (1893) by Bankimchandra Chatterjee in Bangla, *Tara*, subtitled *Kshatra Kula Kamalini* (1902) by Kishorilal Goswami in Hindi, and *Roopnagarchi Rajkanya* (1900–1902) by Harinarain Apte in Marathi.[7] That so many novels of this time chose to deal with Hindu–Mughal conflict was also not an accident; the last Hindu resistance to the Mughal kings came from the Rajputs (and later from Shivaji, another recurrent hero of the historical novels), and fictional representations of their heroism in some way sublimated the present state of subjugation. K.K. Sinha, though not as well known as his Indian-language contemporaries, nevertheless shared with them the teleology of the decline of Hindu glory, in which

Muslim rulers were demonized, carefully shielding the British from blame. Constructing a golden pre-colonial Hindu past was an enterprise implicit in the agenda of nationalism and the spate of historical novels that appeared at the time were a major vehicle for the consolidation of this idea. By imagining or highlighting victories against other and earlier invaders, these novels were helping indirectly to crystallize a sense of pride, through the valorization of both the physical prowess and the spiritual strength of the community. It was largely a masculinist project but women's role was also crucial for defining the ideals of culture and in most of the novels of the time ideal of the *veerangana* (heroic women with agency and power) co-exist — sometimes uncomfortably — with the model of the submissive self-effacing women.[8] Sanjogita who defied her father and ran away with Prithviraj in a soldier's disguise, only to commit sati at her husband's death, was a particularly attractive figure, effecting a synthesis of both these models.

Ten years before *Sanjogita*, K.K. Sinha, once the editor of *The Bihar Guardian* (and incidentally the only Bihari novelist in English I have come across in this early phase) had written a contemporary social novel *The Star of Sikri* (1893) about a Kayastha family at Dinapur. It had a most unlikely theme for its time: a married girl's unrequited love for a man not her husband. The Preface claimed that it was a true story — 'short and correct history of a girl's life' — which could of course be a narrative strategy of the kind Daniel Defoe used in *Robinson Crusoe* or *Moll Flanders*. Surprisingly, instead of censuring Ranjini's unfaithful conduct, this author, whose social and religious orthodoxy is evident in every page of both novels, idealizes this girl's love and even her sexual yearning (e.g. at one point she holds the hand of her beloved's wife and says 'How fortunate is this body which has come in touch with him', p. 70). In a novel set in contemporary India this English-educated gentleman seems ambivalent about Indian women's conduct. At one point he considers it 'downright cruelty [on the father's part] to marry a girl [off] against her opinion' (p. 7), a lesson evidently learnt by reading novels from England where the tension between the society and individual often provided the plot dynamics; and at another point he argues that women should be kept 'within parda, which is ... a matter of pride and pleasure for them' (p. 75); but in the novel set in the twelfth century, all these contradictions get miraculously resolved.

Sanjogita is the ideal woman 'for whom burnt the topless towers of Delhi and Kanauj' (p. 8). She is brave enough to defy her father in choosing Prithviraj at the swayamvara and later running away with him on the same horse in male garb and braving hardship with him during the battle, but diffident enough not to be alone with him before a marriage ceremony could be performed: 'Her sentiments of love were strong, but they could not disregard the prescriptions of religion (p. 175).' Religion is a dominant thread in this story of love and war because, with Prithviraj's death, the fate of Hindu power was 'decided perhaps once for all ... Prithviraj died, and with him died, perhaps the glory or our brilliant past' (p. 254).

The double use of 'perhaps' in one paragraph in the quotation above highlights the dilemma of an Hindu chauvinist author writing in English during the heyday of colonial rule. Should he lament his present status or not? In historical terms the Hindus had been defeated twice over, but the hatred seemed to be directed only to the former Muslim rulers. The Hindi and Bangla historical novels of the time can also be easily accused of communalism because, despite the formation of the Indian National Congress in 1885, the emergent nationalism was for most North Indians still a largely Hindu idea. From *Nihsahay Hindu* (Hindi, 1891) and *Anandamath* (Bangla, 1882) onwards, scores of novels projected the moral superiority of Hindus even though in the battlefield the Muslims vanquished them. But K.K. Sinha, writing in English, also has to grapple with the presence of the Englishman —

probably his immediate target reader. The internal factionalism that made Prithviraj lose to Mohammad Ghori had an exact parallel in the way the British annexed a good part of India, but Sinha ignores it completely to celebrate the presence of the new rulers ('Their [the British] overlordship is absolutely necessary to her [India's] growth and greatness; she cannot possibly do without them', p. 267). Prithviraj's defeat to the Prince of Ghor had a historical lesson, but Sinha highlights only the irrevocable tragedy, and on second thoughts finds final consolation in the excellence of British rule. It would be difficult to locate examples of such abjectness in the novels in the Indian languages, even though many of them also had to navigate in the treacherous terrain between patriotism and expediency.

V

Even though not widely read or discussed, Lal Behari Day and K.K. Sinha at least get brief mentions in the official *History of Indian Literature*, vol. VIII: 1900–1910,[9] Day more than once, with approbation, and Sinha dismissively in half a sentence. But Sarath Kumar Ghosh, the author of *The Prince of Destiny: The New Krishna* (1909) seems to be a truly forgotten writer although his book, in terms of magnitude, philosophical depth and civilizational concerns seems to be a major endeavour. This could be the first serious articulation in fiction of the tension suffered by the early generation of English-educated men in India regarding negotiation of different world views, later glibly and simplistically labelled the 'east-west encounter'.

Unlike Lal Behari Day who has to be seen in the context of Bengal and K.K. Sinha who came from Bihar, a part of the Hindi literary world (Khadagvilas Press in Patna in those days was one of the centres for Hindi publication), it would be difficult to place Ghosh in any specific geographical or linguistic location in India.

Despite his Bengali name, the novel does not indicate that he had his cultural roots in Bengal and I have not been able to find any biographical information about him. The novel was published in London and the Publisher's Preface to the Colonial Edition makes a point about printing the author's photograph wearing a turban in order to assure readers that, in spite of his excellent command of English, he is actually an Indian.[10] The novel is set in a princely state somewhere in north India and although the present-day Bharatpur is situated in Rajasthan, Ghosh's Barathpur (his orthography is different) is evidently an allegorical space which his protagonist has to become worthy of ruling. In this indeterminacy of location, or the projection of 'India' as a trope, a state of mind or a cultural signifier, Sarath Kumar Ghosh is a progenitor of several later Indian novelists in English.

The novel is mainly about the education of prince Barath. He is born on the day Queen Victoria became the Empress of India, which occasioned great show and pageantry in Delhi, thus becoming 'hand-cuffed' to history — as Salman Rushdie's hero would be years later. While a student at Cambridge, Barath would go to London for Victoria's diamond jubilee celebrations and be presented to the queen 'in his resplendent princely attire', thus strengthening the ties with history even further.

Barath's education begins at home under the double tutelage of two gurus — Vashisht, the high priest in the Vishnu temple, and Vishwamitra who worshipped Saraswati. His sister Delini gave him another kind of training, the description of which needs to be quoted at length because the passage ties up with other Indian novels in English in indirect ways:

She taught him the customs of the caste, the language and traditions of the dynasty — aye — the memories and associations of Bharathbarsha. Here, upon this rock sat sorrowful Sita in her weary exile; upon this rose bush was caught Sakuntala's veil ... upon this lotus-bed stood the goddess Saraswati when she inspired the poet Kalidas to write his magic verse. Besides this pool lay love-lorn Prithviraj, Emperor of all India, thinking of his lost bride Sanjogini, and unconsciously feeding the fishes with his necklace of pearls, bead by bead, and here behind him stood, all unknown, Sanjogini herself with veiled face — till reading the proof of his love in his absorption she handed him over her necklace when his own had come to an end, just to revel a little longer in the proof of his love. All these memories Delini taught her little brother. For in India almost every grove and glade, pool and rivulet, valley and mountain is associated with the history of a demigod. (p. 34)

Apart from the last lines of this passage prefiguring Raja Rao's idea on *sthalapurana* being an essential ingredient of traditional history, as stated in his Foreword to *Kanthapura*, they also remind us of Krupa Satthianadhan's evocation (in *Saguna* and *Kamala*) of stories that connect specific natural spots to puranic lore in the remotest parts of India: 'this is Seeta's bath, and the rude slab of rock cut in the shape of a cot ... is the cradle of her babe' (*Kamala*, p. 74). The reference to Prithviraj above repeats almost exactly an episode described in detail in K.K. Sinha's novel just discussed, testifying to the popularity of the Sanjogita story at that time. All the references touch upon a common memory, an emotional idea of India and the common culture that binds it together, without any intervention of the local or the particular, a mind-set not unknown among the English writers in our country, even today.

The *Prince of Destiny* is an 'Indian' novel, in the way *The Serpent and the Rope* or *Midnight's Children* are Indian, because they are all concerned with defining, constructing or interrogating the idea of India. But it is also set on a global stage where not only England, but Italy and Japan play a part. In the Suez Canal, on his way to Europe, Barath came across a shipload of 13,000 Italian youths bound for the war in Abyssinia where they were eventually to be defeated. Barath takes upon himself the role of preparing them for the battle by shouting 'Long Live Italy!'

Why should he not cry for the long life of Italy? To him and to the world Italy meant something more than the triumph of war ... Yes, he would cry "Long Live Italy!". That would be his greeting to Europe.

Thus the thirteen thousand Italian boys were shouting to their death at the call of this Hindu boy. Why not? Krishna himself had exhorted Arjuna and his warriors on the day before the great battle of the Mahabharata. (p. 134)

This is even before he reaches Europe where he learns to be part of a greater world and yet retain his own identity. Years later as the ruler of Barathpur he has to deal with a web of political forces working on him — the nationalists, militant religious groups, terrorists from Bengal and British forces ready to appropriate his kingdom. There is also the pull of Japan as the counterforce to Europe.

Barath's traditional education at home would not have equipped him with knowledge to grapple with all this. In order to learn statecraft and *kshatriya dharma* he had to be sent out early in life. At Raj Kumars' College in Ajmere his friends tried to make a man out of him by initiating him into hunting, but the first animal he wounded brought about a spiritual crisis intended to remind the reader of Valmiki's transformation. This was one of the early indications of his destiny.

At Cambridge he studied mathematics and got curious about the point where it converged with philosophy. His reading of English history, his friendship with writers like Francis Thompson, with whom he nightly wandered the streets of London, his love for an archetypical English girl Nora and attachment to an English family where he found a mother substitute — all contribute towards an understanding of another culture. He returns to deal with the complex realities of his native state, but all through his involvement in its development and participation in its politics he is beset by metaphysical questions. The two women in his life — Nora the English girl, and Sumona the princess he is betrothed to marry — stand for symbolic options in a philosophical choice — much like what Ramaswamy in Raja Rao's *The Serpent and the Rope* or Krishnan in B. Rajan's *The Dark Dancer* had faced at a later date. It is amazing how the east–west alternatives tend to operate through the emblematic figures of women in Indian fiction in English. In novels not in English, these choices are never posited in such clear-cut terms.

Barath's choice however, one has to admit, is not quite a clear-cut one — neither politically nor philosophically. Nora goes back, realizing that Sumona's claims are greater. Barath marries Sumona but also teaches her the path of renunciation. There is no conventional happiness at the end of the novel. Leaving Sumona to rule the state on behalf of their son (adopted from another royal family so that the lineage remains pure) Barath becomes a sanyasi:

Barath went out of the palace, into the world ... Search for him ... somewhere between the upper Ganges and Boddh Gaya, or between Benares and Nasik. Somewhere there you will find him sitting beneath a bodhi tree, awaiting his call. The New Krishna has not come, for indeed Barath was not he; but the world may hope for a New Buddha ... (p. 629)

These little-known novels of an earlier era can become case studies of various kinds: to explore if the English language imposes certain compulsions in the way experience is processed (see for example how each of the three novels refer to or describe or reflect on the practice of sati), or are the individual differences more overriding than the common features of the category? What is their relationship with the literary productions of the same age written in Indian languages?

Notes

1. Some of these pre-novel texts in Bangla are *Kolikata Kamalalay* (1820) by Bhabanicharan Bandopadhyay, *Babur Upakhyan* (1821) published in two parts anonymously in *Samachar Darpan*, *Nabababubilas* (1825) by Bhabanicharan Bandopadhyay, *Alaler Gharer Dulal* (1858) by Pyarichand Mitra, *Hutom Pyanchar Naksha* by Kali Prasanna Singha.

2. I am indebted to Shubhendu Kumar Mund who drew my attention to these two pieces and made one available to me. For detailed discussion of

early English novels in India see his book *The Indian Novel in English: Its Birth and Development* (New Delhi and Bhubaneshwar: Prachi Prakashan, 1997).

3. And shall we, shall men, after five and twenty years of ignominious servitude, shall we, through a fear of dying defer one single instant to assert our liberty? No, Romans, now is the time; the favourable moment we have been waiting for is come.

—Junius Brutus

4. *The Works of Soshee Chunder Dutt* in six volumes (London: Lovell Reeve & Co., 1884).

5. Thomas Babington Macaulay, 'Minute on Indian Education', *Victorian Prose*, ed. S. Nagarajan, *et al.* (Poona: University of Poona Publication, 1968), p. 71.

6. O. Chandu Menon, *Indulekha*, 1889, translated by W. Dumergue (Calicut, 1890, rpt. 1965), p. xiv. I have read only the English translation.

7. James Tod, *Annals and Antiquities of Rajasthan* (London, 1929; rpt. New Delhi, 1978), vol. I, p. 301.

8. For further discussion see my piece 'Story, History and Her Story', *Studies in History*, 9, 1, ns, 1993, pp. 71–85.

9. *A History of Indian Literature*, vol. VIII, 1800–1910, ed. Sisir Kumar Das (New Delhi: Sahitya Akademi, 1991).

10. ... When the author of this romance finished his education in Great Britain and began his literary career, his style and action were so pure as to cause an eminent English critic to say that many distinguished English novelists might well envy him his command of English prose. Nay a leading London review averred, "We cannot be persuaded to believe that Mr Sarath Kumar Ghosh is anything but an Englishman in masquerade". In view of that the publishers of this romance deemed it expedient to present the author's portrait in the British edition in a dress representative of India, in order to convince readers that he is truly Indian.

Publisher's Preface, *Prince of Destiny*, London, 1909.

4

Ambiguous Discourse:
The Novels of Krupa
Satthianadhan

> I had chafed under the restraints and the ties which
> formed the common lot of women, and I longed for
> an opportunity to show that a woman is in no way
> inferior to a man. How hard it seemed to my mind that
> marriage should be the goal of women's ambition, and
> that she should spend her days in the light trifles of a
> home life, live to dress, to look pretty and never know
> the joy of independence and intellectual work. The
> thought had been galling. It made me avoid men, and
> I felt more than once that I could not look into their
> faces unless I was able to hold my own with them.

The passage above might well have been an extract from *Jane
Eyre*, the heroine protesting against the stifling conditions of
her life — a companion piece perhaps to her silent scream of
rebellion in chapter X: 'I desired liberty; for liberty I uttered a
prayer; it seemed scattered on the wind then faintly blowing' —
lines foregrounded today in most feminist readings of the novel.

As it happens, however, the lines are actually from a novel titled

Saguna, published in Madras in 1895, written by an Indian woman much acclaimed in the prefatory pages for her piety and Christian virtue. The name of Krupa Satthianadhan (1862–94) is not quite unknown to those who delve in the history of Indian writing in English because her two novels *Saguna* and *Kamala* are listed in almost all books on the subject, beginning with K.R. Srinivasa Iyengar's first study in 1943, and she is generally cited, along with Toru Dutt, Raj Lakshmi Debi and Shevantibai Nikambe, as an example of Indian women who wrote novels in English in the nineteenth century.[1] These bibliographical entries have for decades been carried over from one literary history to another, without any scholar attempting to analyse the texts, let alone detect any proto-feminist chinks in the seemingly solid walls of their irreproachable propriety.

Many years ago while doing my doctoral research on Indian novels in English, I abandoned the search for these early texts to focus on a later period, because the libraries I then had access to (including the National Library in Calcutta) did not have copies of these rare books. I must confess that the drab documentary subtitles of Satthianadhan's novels — 'A Story of Native Christian Life' and 'A Story of Hindu Life' did not encourage me to actively continue the pursuit of these books in subsequent years. My interest in Krupa Satthianadhan was rekindled after reading an extract from *Saguna* in the first volume of *Women Writing in India* (1990) edited by Susie Tharu and K. Lalita. This witty and ironic piece brought her alive momentarily, but did not quite prepare me for the richness, intensity and fascinating contradictions of her two novels — which took me by surprise when I finally found them.[2]

Daughter of a brahman scholar who converted to Christianity long before her birth, Krupa grew up in western Maharashtra and came to Madras to study medicine, where she also met her future husband Samuel Satthianadhan. She could not complete her course because of her poor health, but began writing articles

for newspapers from different towns of south India — Ootaca-
mund, Rajahmundry and Kumbakonam — where her husband's
work took them. Before she died at Conoor at the age of thirty-
two, one of her novels was published, the other appeared posthumously.[3] The first, titled *Saguna, A Story of Native Christian Life*,
serialized in the *Madras Christian College Magazine* in the late
1880s and published as a book in 1895, and the other *Kamala, A
Story of Hindu Life* (1895), were both brought out in hard covers
by a Madras-based publishing house Srinivasa Varadachari and
Co., and never again reprinted in the entire century that intervened, until 1998, when these two novels appeared in the Classic
Re-issue series of Oxford University Press. Chandini Lokuge, who
edited these, has attempted to situate the novels in the current
academic discourse, emphasizing in her Introductions the aspects
that would engage the attention of feminist and post-colonial
readers.

The flat descriptive sub-titles of the original editions that belie
the liveliness and intensity of the actual narratives (Lokuge in the
new reprint changes one of them) are part of the legacy Satthianadhan inherited from her other nineteenth-century Indian English
literary ancestors who seemed always eager to promise glimpses
into 'native' life. Like her predecessors, Krupa Satthianadhan can
also be read as a mediator offering 'authentic' representations of a
life to which the British would forever remain outsiders. I choose
not to attempt that reading here — a deliberate decision arrived
at as a reaction to the lengthy Forewords, Prefaces and Introductions added to the original editions of both the novels where
various Englishwomen — Mrs Grigg, Mrs Benson, etc., whoever
they be (possibly wives of the District Collector and the Director
of Public Instructions), have certified to the fine quality of Satthianadhan's English and praised the way 'she has interpreted her
countrywoman to us as no writer has done before'.[4] Eulogistic
reviews from British periodicals and Anglo-Indian newspapers are

extensively quoted at the end. *Malabar and Travancore Spectator* said: 'As we read, we fancy it is some English lady who has written the book, so charming it is to us.' That Queen Victoria should actually read the first volume and like it well enough to ask for the second is seen as the highest possible plaudit for this young Indian writer. The physical get-up of the two volumes — the text sand-wiched between hagiographies of the virtuous author which inform us *who* she is, and the reviews telling us *how* to read her novels, indicate a tendency towards appropriation.

Cutting through this patronizing verbiage of the colonial as well as the missionary variety (one praising her skill in the English language and the other extolling her Christian piety), I would like to place Krupa Satthianadhan in three indigenous contexts — one: as an early Indian novelist to be seen in relation to writers in other Indian languages; two: as a woman writer, the author of what may well be the first two female bildungsromans written in our sub-continent; three: as part of a Christian tradition of writing rooted in India if such a tradition can be constructed. Before expanding on these three contexts, which incidentally intersect at many points, a brief description of the two novels is perhaps necessary because, given the century of inaccessibility, familiarity with the texts cannot be presupposed.

Despite the difference in social milieu represented in the two novels — one Christian, the other Hindu, largely brahman — both deal with a common theme: the growing into womanhood of two girls who feel trapped in the standard mould of domesticity. Kamala and Saguna are both fond of books and face varying degrees of hostility and ridicule for such an unnatural inclination. *Saguna* is largely autobiographical and, despite many odds, as the daughter of a Christian convert the protagonist manages not only to receive formal education, but also to get admission into a medical college, and eventually meet a man who would share her life on an equal basis.

Kamala's life follows a different trajectory altogether. Daughter of a learned sanyasi, she is brought up in a sparsely-populated hilly area, innocent of the narrowly caste-bound and intrigue-ridden community into which she is married. Reminiscent of the epony-mous heroine of Bankimchandra Chattopadhyay's Bangla novel *Kapalakundala* (1866), who too was brought up outside the stratified and gender-oppressive upper-caste Hindu joint family by a sanyasi in a forest, and who dared to say 'Had I known marriage turns a woman into a bonded slave I would not have married',[5] Kamala does not understand the behavioural norms of the world her marriage has thrown her into, and despite her best efforts re-mains a misfit. Her happiest moments are when her father-in-law allows her to handle and arrange his books, or when her husband during a brief radical phase in his life gives her lessons in reading and writing against the wishes of his mother. These joys turn out to be short-lived; the joint family mounts a collective campaign to rub off the individual edges of Kamala's inquiring spirit. It is a familiar story retold many times in nineteenth-century autobiog-raphies by Indian women.[6] In the ethos of the joint family women's reading was seen as subversive activity as it fostered a desire for privacy and engendered a spirit of individualism — both tenden-cies were suspect because they were linked with selfishness and a betrayal of the group ethos. By the end of the novel Kamala's unfaithful husband dies of cholera, freeing her from marital bond-age, and her long-time admirer from a distance, her father's disciple, is willing to give up sanyas to marry her. The Christian author, who might have found this marriage an acceptable happy ending at a time when widow marriage had legal sanction as well, nevertheless desists from granting this easy solution to her brah-man heroine, making her opt for living alone to work for the poor in the village. The last lines of the novel tell us that, when she died, there 'were a shrine and a chhutram bearing the name of Kamala, who had now become a saint. Her unseen hands still relieve the poor and protect the unfortunate; for she left her fortune for the sole benefit of widows and orphans.' This ending raises certain theoretical issues about the closure of woman-centred novels in general — to which I shall return later.

Contrary to the expectations aroused by the Christian missionaries' claim of the religious ardour of the author, the two novels do not turn out to be polemical in tone or content. There is no overt extolling of the liberatory potential of Christianity, nor condemnation of the traditional Hindu way of life. If the child-bride Kamala is miserable in her husband's house, we find similar tales of woe in many Bangla or Marathi novels of the time written by authors who are very much part of the Hindu ethos, the most remarkable example being Harinarain Apte's *Pan Lakshyant Kon Gheto* (1890). Despite an awareness of gender and caste iniquity inherent in the practice of traditional brahmanism, Satthianadhan does not articulate these issues directly in terms of religion. Chandani Lokuge in a paper published in 1992 had read these two novels as part of a continuous argument — one propagating Christianity and the western model of individualism for women in India, the other exposing the gender exploitation intrinsic to Hindu society.[7] Her 1998 Introductions are more nuanced, but the central statement does not alter substantially. This simple schematic reading elides the dialogic tensions set up in both the novels between religious dogma and independent questioning, between rigid social hierarchy and fluid identity, between colonial education and traditional wisdom, and between individual agency and the power of the community which can be alternatively nurturing or claustrophobic. The rites and rituals, myths and legends that permeate rural life in Hindu communities, instead of being rejected as superstitious, are described in a language evocative enough to contain anticipatory echoes of Raja Rao's *Kanthapura* (1938), well known for lyrically merging myth and history, for conflating the sacred and the political to evoke the spirit of a place and the mental world of its inhabitants.

Here for example is the description of a pilgrimage Kamala undertakes to Dudhasthala, where the Ganga and the Godavari converge to leap down from a huge rock to a cavern below: 'This is Seeta's bath, and the rude slab of rock cut in the shape of a cot with moss-grown stones underneath ... is the cradle of her babe. A tree cut by a reckless woodman's axe shows signs of the god's presence ... for a god has visited the place.' (p. 74) Compare this with the opening lines from the famous Foreword to *Kanthapura* by Raja Rao to see how closely both the authors empathize with the mythical imagination of village people:

There is no village in India, however mean, that has not a rich sthalapu-rana, or legendary history, of its own. Some god or godlike hero has passed by the village — Rama might have rested under this pipal-tree, Sita might have dried her clothes after her bath on this yellow stone ... [8]

Not only *Kamala*, purportedly a 'story of Hindu life', where such passages may appear as natural parts of the ethos, but *Saguna*, 'a Story of Native Christian Life', also contains similar passages. A landscape of awesome craggy grandeur in western Maharashtra is described thus:

There was a well-known tradition to the effect that part of the country was haunted. And indeed what is not haunted in India? Every grove has its spirit, every stream its nymph or naiad, every dark spot its ghost, and every hill its goddess or ruling deity. (p. 8)

This acknowledges the importance of *sthalapuranas* in chronicling regional history. But for the reference to the nymphs or naiads which are evidently products of the author's exposure to English literature, there is nothing here that distances the reader from local thought processes. Krupa Satthianadhan continues: 'But this was the abode of the ghost of a real suttee who had lived and died in the place' nearly a hundred years ago. Then she goes off at a tangent to relate the story of a woman burnt on her husband's funeral pyre, which seems to me not a digression at all but a reaffirmation of one of the author's central concerns that forms the common sub-text of her two novels, namely society's fear and anxiety about women's empowerment through education.

The legend about the sati goes like this: about a hundred years ago a girl-bride was married to a rich old banker in a nearby village. She happened to have been taught by her father to read and write, a skill considered unnatural and inauspicious in a woman. When her husband died, she was perceived as a sorceress and pressurized into climbing onto his pyre. While the two bodies perfumed with camphor and sandalwood were about to be burnt amidst deafening music, 'Suddenly a form was seen to bound through the fire and rush out with a shriek. The people in alarm fell back, and the form fled screaming to the hills. None had the courage to pursue it.' (p. 10)

One does not know if Krupa Satthianadhan had any access to the contemporary eyewitness accounts of actual cases of widow-burning, but there is an uncanny resemblance between her account of a legend and the descriptions of actual widows who were often reported to have fled from the pyre when the flames hit their body. Lata Mani in her oft-cited study of these eyewitness accounts writes: 'In most descriptions of sati, as the widow ascends the pyre, the details vanish almost as magically, it would seem, as the narrator would have us believe that the widow herself evaporates.' She quotes from an actual eyewitness description: 'in a moment the soul of the devoted girl fled in shrieks to the world of spirit.'[9] The key words — shriek, fled and spirit — link the narration of the legend in *Saguna* to the eyewitness account of a real historical event. The sati in the Satthianadhan novel — or her spirit — remained in the forest, lived on in stories told in hushed voices, and was rumoured to have been occasionally glimpsed by the shepherds. It seems to me, she also lives on in the novels of Krupa Satthianadhan, lurking between the pages of these apparently realistic tales of modern times, an uncomfortable reminder of the perpetually peripheral position of a woman who dared to be different.

Whether she be a Christian Saguna or a brahman Kamala, she is an embarrassment to those around her. Saguna's anxious mother brings her apologetically to a girls' boarding school: 'My daughter is alone at home. She learns a little too much, so I have brought her here to be more like other girls' (p. 169), and Kamala's illiterate mother-in-law sends her away to her parental home hoping never to see her:

As for me I am fairly tired of that girl. She causes much disturbance when here ... what with her mad fits of learning ... I really wish that she was not returning at all. Such a responsibility too, and not at all like the other girls. She knows no work to be in any way useful, and when scolded instead of sulking like other girls she says that everything is her fault and that she will do better. (p. 140)

She does not fit the assumptions of patriarchy that women should be either passive objects of pleasure and convenience, or creatures intriguing for domestic power. How can such odd women be socially integrated? This has been the question at the heart of many female bildungsromans in different cultures. Other women writers have grappled with this dilemma before Satthianadhan, as Charlotte Bronte did with Jane Eyre and George Eliot with Maggie Tulliver and Dorothea Brooke in Victorian England. Since the institution of marriage was by nature unequal, the taming of a free spirit in marriage often left the reader unsatisfied even when the formal requirements of a happy ending were met.

II

In the second part of the essay I return to the three overlapping contexts in which I intend to place Krupa Satthianadhan. She was not the first woman in India to write novels; in Bangla she was preceded by Swarnakumari Debi (1856–1932) whose novels *Deep-nirban* (An Extinguished Lamp, 1870) and *Chhinna-mukul* (A Plucked Bud, 1879) were published two decades before *Saguna* and *Kamala*, and Swarnakumari's other novels *Virodh* (Conflict, 1890) and *Snehalata ba Palita* (Snehalata or The Adopted One, in two volumes, 1892 and 1893), were roughly contemporary with Satthianadhan's work. But there is no evidence that the latter writer knew of the former's existence, because the only novel by Swarnakumari to be translated into English, *Kahake?* (To Whom?, 1898; in English translation *The Unfinished Song*), was written after the death of Krupa Satthianadhan. In English Raj Lakshmi Debi's *The Hindoo Wife or The Enchanted Fruit* was published in 1876 and Toru Dutt's *Bianca, The Young Spanish Maiden* was serialized in 1878 — but all these were unconnected events. Women's writing was not a continuous tradition at that time.

Even in novels written by men, women had figured centrally in early Indian fiction, ranging from *Durgeshnandini* and *Kapalkundala* (1866) to *Chokher Bali* (1903, translated into English as *Binodini*) in Bangla, *Indulekha* (1889) and *Sukumari* (1897) in Malayalam, *Indirabai* (1899) and *Vagdevi* (1903) in Kannada, *Devrani Jethani ki Kahani* (1866) and *Umrao Jan Ada* (1899) in Hindi and Urdu respectively, among many others. I have elsewhere speculated at length on this conjunction between women and the new genre (not only in India, but in England too, where the novel emerged as a popular form a century earlier) — the woman becoming both the site and the source of a transition from the feudal to a capitalist/colonial way of life and the representational shift that coincided with it.[10]

The question of women and their agency figured prominently in the realist novel of the nineteenth century, and a writer like Bankimchandra handled it by creating a new order of women outside the enclosed space of domesticity who could broadly be categorized as *veerangana* (the warrior woman) — e.g. Debi Chaudhurani, the bandit queen for example, or Shanti in *Anandamath* who fought the British invaders alongside men. They could be granted freedom and power so long as they remained in the hills, forests, lonely beaches and battlefields, outside the conjugal domain — spatially as well as socially. But within the walls of the household a woman's code of conduct was different. The passionate and transgressive women in Bankim's corpus — Matangini, Shaibalini, Rohini — like Subhadra in C.V. Raman Pillai's Malayalam novel *Marthanda Varma* (1891) have to be relentlessly punished at the end in order to uphold social stability, even though the author and the reader may understand and admire their rebellion. In many nineteenth-century novels, not only in Bangla but also in some of the Marathi and Malayalam novels I have read in translation, women's agency is foregrounded, but with a simultaneous reminder of its disruptive social potential. The freedom achieved outside the domestic enclosure was purchased at the risk of ostracism, or at best marginalization, while paradoxi-cally a central position in society — as a wife or a mother — could be granted to only those who submitted to the collective feminine code of conformity which erased the individual self.

How does Krupa Satthianadhan negotiate a space for her heroines who are not so much transgressive as misfits in a conven-tional society? That their 'aberrations' are not sexual but intellec-tual make it easier for them to gain the reader's sympathy than might be accorded to a more passionate heroine. The nearest to erotic desire in her novels is the attraction Kamala's friend Bhagi-rathi feels for a man who is not her husband. Bhagirathi's own husband has not been faithful and, when approached by a man who makes her feel desired, her first impulse is to yield, but it is Kamala who reasons with her against succumbing to this tempta-tion, and she does so empirically, without adopting a moral tone. Female bonding and mutual counselling among the young ex-ploited wives provides a down-to-earth ballast in the novel to the high romance of illicit passion.

But the dialectic between outdoor landscape and enclosed space operates in Satthianadhan's novels too. The vast open Deccan

plateau where both the heroines grow up serves as the prelapsarian
space of innocence and freedom, to act as a counterpoint to the
meanness of the crowded lives within houses in the plains. Travel
serves an important function in the narrative. Fugitive from so-
cietal persecution for having married for love, Kamala's parents
traversed a sacred geography on the way to Kashi, being supremely
happy in the simple life lived in the forest under the sky, almost
like Rama and Sita during their exile. Kamala's father recounts
those days to her daughter thus:

> Your mother read with me, with bewildered eyes, books that are never
> put into women's hands, and she was delighted when difficult portions
> were explained. Nothing came between her and me and as her under-
> standing unfolded, her love for me increased. Is it any wonder then that
> I love the mountains and the woods? They were kinder to us than human
> beings. (p. 151)

Reading that was forbidden for women could be undertaken only
in the forest with impunity. From Pandita Ramabai Saraswati's
autobiographical account *My Testimony* we learn that before her
birth in 1858 there was consternation in the community because
her father had wanted to teach her mother Sanskrit. He could do
it only when he decided to leave his village to live in 'a place in a
dense forest on the top of a peak of the Western Ghat' where no
one would censor him for this heretical act.[11] One of the best moments in Kamala's own adult life, normally spent under the strict
surveillance of her mother and sisters-in-law, was the pilgrimage
to Dudhasthal — the journey providing her contact with the
universe outside the narrow confines of home, with the hills and
the river and the forest. 'Kamala cared not what her sisters-in-law
thought of her. They were there, but they had no power over her'
(p. 71). Even when back in the village, the stolen happy hours
Kamala has with her friends — four young married girls, all
oppressed by their mothers-in-law to a greater or lesser degree —
are always outdoors, at the river bank, or under a tree — never

within the four walls of a house. These interludes of fun and laughter and their playful mockery of their oppressors save the girls from being stereotypical victim figures, embodying as they do an irrepressible life-force that resists familial cruelty. As in many other nineteenth-century novels, nature thus forms an important structural motif — not merely a decorative one, as Satthianadhan's English reviewers who praise her nature descriptions seemed to think. If the travels of Kamala and her parents take them across sacred space, Saguna's travel is along the axis of colonial geography — from Nasik to a Christian village Vishrampur and then to Bombay and eventually, when her hopes of going to England are thwarted, from Bombay by train alone to Madras to study in a medical college. Journeys and relocations provide the dynamics of change in Saguna's life, externally as well as intellectually.

This novel contains a long and detailed account of Saguna's brahman father's voluntary conversion to Christianity and the emotional crisis accompanying the event. I have not read any other fictional account that goes into the subjectivity of both the introspective man for whom it is an act of faith and the unwilling wife who has to choose between the husband and the most secure foundations of her life. The only other account to describe a similar tension between personal faith and wifely duty can be found in Lakshmibai Tilak's (1868–1936) autobiography written much later — (*Smruti Chitre*, Marathi, 1936; available in English translation in a truncated version as *I Follow After*, 1951, reprinted 1998). Narayan Waman Tilak, a poet and thinker, converted to Christianity in 1895, causing an upheaval in the extended family and completely traumatizing his devoted wife — who nearly lost her sanity. Incidentally, Lakshmibai was living at that time in the same geographical region where Krupabai and her two heroines, Saguna and Kamala grew up — near Nasik in Maharashtra, by the river Godavari. When Lakshmibai's brother came to look for Tilak, he refused to go home:

Tilak said, "I have have become a Christian. Look after your sister. The river Godavari runs by both Nasik and Jalalpur. See that she does not commit suicide."[12]

Lakshmibai did contemplate suicide, first in the Godavari then in the well in the backyard, but desisted for fear of further sullying the family honour. She wept continuously for months, stopped talking to people and became a nervous wreck. Reconciliation with her husband took several years and finally she too converted to Christianity in 1900. Lakshmibai's story parallels Saguna's mother Radhabai's troubled life with her converted husband. Virtually kidnapped by her Christian husband, whom she hardly knew, Radhabai found his new way of life intolerable, but was constrained to stay with him because the court had decreed so. Brought up from childhood to fit traditional familial roles as daughter, wife and mother, she suddenly found herself in a lonely situation without a script where she would have to make her own moves. 'She was rebellious and uncontrollable for a long time. She had her idols, kept her fasts and festivals and gave her husband food outside the house' (p. 67). But eventually, like Lakshmibai Tilak, Radhabai came around to her husband's way of thinking and set up a Christian household.

The author of *Saguna*, like its heroine, was the thirteenth child of a brahman father who had been driven by spiritual curiosity to embrace Christianity. Such conversions were less common than those of lower-caste people who often opted for conversion to gain social status or economic advantage. Like many first novels by women, *Saguna* seems closely autobiographical,[13] and from the meagre details of the author's life available to us it is difficult to sift the fictional from the factual. It may not thus be entirely irrelevant to compare *Saguna* with other life-stories like Lakshmibai Tilak's *Smruti Chitre* or with Pandita Ramabai Saraswati's *My Testimony*, a brief but vivid and moving autobiography, which too, like *Saguna*, was unfortunately 'too strongly promoted as a

Christian tract' to find 'a place among the literary masterpieces of the period'.[14]

Because many of the so-called 'Christian' narratives of the nineteenth century were directly propagandist, the nuanced and complex work by Pandita Ramabai or Krupabai's novels with their unexpected contradictions have tended to become flattened in people's minds by association. In very few of the early Christian novels in India for example — *Yamuna Paryatan* (1857) in Marathi, *Prathapa Muddaliar Charitram* (1879) in Tamil, *Sukumari* (1897) in Malayalam or *Phulmoni O Karunar Bibaran* (1852) in Bangla — do we have any record of the spiritual and social tensions and the conflict of loyalties that an individual might experience at the moment of conversion. Two other Christian novelists of the nineteenth century are mentioned by Krishna Chaitanya in *A History of Malayalam Literature*, Kochuthomman and Kocheeppan Tharakan, but they too, we are told, 'avoided raising problems' and limited themselves to simple descriptions of middle-class Christian life.[15] *Saguna* does not hesitate to raise problems, and becomes a full-fledged novel instead of being a mere tract because conversion is seen here not only as a redemptive act for Saguna's father who could not find the answers he was looking for in brahamanic scriptures, but also as a disturbing one for those around him. His mother, so far presented in the novel as an affectionate and reasonable woman, becomes ready to poison her son rather than suffer the indignity of excommunication that his conversion would bring to the family.

The author's own faith in Christianity may have been firm, but as a novelist she was not averse to expressing her heroine's doubts and misgivings. The Bible preaches equality for all, but missionaries made a distinction between British and Indians. Intrepid as she was, Saguna spoke up against such anomaly and was duly reprimanded. When the Christian missions in India appropriated Krupa Satthianadhan's work, such uncomfortable moments were conveniently glossed over in their lavish praise for the ideal native Christian woman.

Even though neither Saguna nor her creator was as learned in theological matters as Pandita Ramabai Saraswati (1858–1922), who had opted to become a Christian after studying the Vedas and the Upanishads, one recalls in this connection Ramabai's differences with Christian priests over religious dogma:

> I am, it is true, a member of the church of Christ, but I am not bound to accept every word that falls from the lips of priests and bishops ... Obedience to the Word of God is quite different from perfect obedience to priests only. I have just, with great effort, freed myself from the yoke of the Indian priestly tribe, so I am not at present willing to place myself under another similar yoke.[16]

While giving an account of Pandita Ramabai's 'volatile relation' with the Anglican Church in the nineteenth century, 'which was patriarchal and racist', Uma Chakravarti argues that one of the reasons why the life and works of such an important activist have been 'marginalised from mainstream history' is that 'colonial patriarchy interlocked with indigenous patriarchy' to suppress a dissenting female voice. Also, because in the last decades of the nineteenth century the 'nation' had come to be viewed 'in terms of a predominantly Hindu ethos, there has been a certain ambiguity about Ramabai's place in Indian society'.[17]

There is an implicit debate in the novel *Saguna* about the relationship between Christianity and Indian nationalism. When Saguna's father wanted to become a Christian, the arguments put forward to dissuade him were not all religious in nature: 'One objection to the religion of Christ was that it was foreign, the religion of the conquerors, and therefore it was very unpatriotic for an orthodox Hindu to exchange it for his own faith'. (p. 58) Harichander was of course proof against this argument. 'Patriotism that sacrificed truth to blind sentiments, was, he said, no true patriotism'. (p. 58)

Indeed there is no one more patriotic in the novel than the good Christian Saguna, who upbraids a fashionable foreign-returned young Indian for talking of England as 'home', and finds it absurd that a girl who has read too many English novels should confuse her Indian reality with the England of fiction. This girl who referred to her parents as 'pa' and 'ma' explained 'with an air of importance for my benefit' how young ladies wearing 'long trains' and not short skirts 'are taken into society'. To this Saguna's wry comments are:

Like many a novel-reading girl, she lived in a world of her own making and enjoyed it. She knew that the native Christian community was very small, and that there was no society to speak of, neither long skirts not short skirts. Her mother wore a sari. (p. 97)

Physically frail, but intellectually intense, Saguna carries out a single-handed crusade against such false perceptions. She imbibed her nationalistic zeal from a much-admired elder brother Bhaskar, an ardent Christian, who died early:

He talked of doing great things, and forgetting that I was a mere girl, pointed out the ambition of his life and grew eloquent over the great work that had to be done for India. He was a brahman, he said, a brahman to the backbone, and he would show his countrymen what it is to be a real patriot, to live and die for his native land ... He stopped, and looking into my eyes said, and you will help me? Won't you? You will speak to your countrywomen, and be as your sister was, modest, gentle and kind, a real woman. (p. 11)

The intriguing claim to brahmanhood by a devout Christian can be understood perhaps as a pre-emptive denial of the possible charge of a rupture with the spirit of the nation. The words 'brah man', 'patriot' and 'Indian' get inexplicably aligned in Bhaskar's thinking. The blue-print of an ideal womanhood he envisages for his sister, however, invests Indianness with Christian qualities.

The merging of Christianity with the Indian ethos which the above passage implies can be countered with several quotations from the novel where a predictable missionary rhetoric is used to demonstrate how 'the sunbeams of Christianity dispel the darkness of superstition'. Even though most of the time Hindu rituals and festivals are described from an insider's point of view, there are moments when the gaze turns critical, as for example when the Hindu chariot procession is condemned as 'monstrous' and 'barbaric'. Yet in the very next page a moving story is narrated about how the god's chariot refused to move until the poorest of the poor were brought in to participate. (p. 45)

These paradoxes and contradictions make it necessary that Krupa Satthianadhan's texts be sometimes read against the grain. While *Saguna* contains a direct feminist manifesto of the militant variety quoted at the beginning of this essay, Kamala's refusal to remarry at the end problematizes the notion of happy ending by privileging the community over the individual. While Saguna battles against all odds to get admission into a medical college, in *Kamala*, on the whole, in the debate between new learning and old the author's implicit sympathy seems to be with traditional systems. Kamala's husband receives an English education and for a brief period at least, it teaches him the ideal of companionate marriage. The new ideas, however, do not last long because western education has affected him only superficially. Having lost the ethical moorings that his Sanskritist father had, he is soon adrift in a life of profligacy and pleasure. As the immediate reward of colonial education he gets a government job and takes Kamala with him to set up a nuclear family, a marker of modernity. But his bringing home a mistress militates against the basis of this modernity where marriage is predicated upon an ideal of equal partnership. Kamala chooses to return to the joint family in a moment of crisis, not to assert her individuality, but to reclaim her share in the life of the community which can offer support and succour to all its members. The misery she had experienced there earlier is not repeated, because by a Jane-Eyre-like stroke of fairy-tale good fortune, Kamala by now finds herself to be an heiress.

This fairy-tale device is part of a romance narrative that erupts now and then to deflect .the realist account of Kamala's life. Her mother, we learn in a flashback, was a princess sequestered in a fortress until her father married her secretly, and her casket of jewellery which Kamala should have inherited reached her late through a circuitous route. Sai, an unusual female character of limitless freedom and energy who enthrals Kamala's husband, also partially belongs to this romance world. She is a powerful woman — an actress as well as a *veerangana* — who commands the allegiance of the Bheels in the hilly region, has mysterious knowledge of all the robberies that take place in the area and such is her fame that 'even the Government officials consulted her now and then.' (p. 90). She flits in and out of the domestic narrative, destroying Kamala's happiness, but cannot be contained by the demands of realism. Ramchunder, Kamala's secret admirer — another figure from the world of romance — appears off and on in the story, sometimes in a mendicant's garb, sometimes as a physician, and provides an element of suspense in this plain tale of domestic misery.

At the end of the novel there is a chance of a new beginning for Kamala. Her father's disciple Ramchunder, who had always loved her from a distance, steps in, wanting to take her away from society's restrictive demands: 'It is the land of freedom I want you to come to ... We shall create a world of our own where none dare interrupt our joys' (p. 206). Her refusal to be seduced by this romantic utopia-for-two may be read in several ways. It may indicate Kamala's reluctance to forego the sense of security that a community provides; or it may reveal the author's unwillingness to force a radical ending. In the tussle between the romantic and the realist narratives it also marks the triumph of the latter. Alternatively, this may be read as a truly feminist ending where a woman's happiness is not necessarily dependent on her relation-ship with a man. Financially independent at last, and freed of her role as a wife and a mother, Kamala can now choose an active public life of service and responsibility rather than a private one of conjugal bliss.

Opinions are likely to remain divided on whether Satthianadhan should be considered a feminist before her time or a staid conform-ist; a realist or a romancer; a propagator of social emancipation through Christianity or a nostalgic evacuator of the timeless past of legends myths and rituals. This indeterminacy results in deferred climaxes and invests her novels with an uneven texture. But it also makes them fertile sites for generating multiple interpretations. It is this ambiguous configuration between the predictable and the unexpected that makes Krupa Satthianadhan's imperfect novels such fascinating cultural documents, suggesting different ways of reading which may not be contained neatly in the simple binary grid of tradition/modernity or individualism/collective identity — the grids through which nineteenth-century India has generally been studied.

Notes

1. M.K. Naik, *History of Indian Writing in English* (New Delhi: Sahitya Akademi, 1981).

2. I am grateful to Priya Joshi, Department of English, University of California, Berkeley, for sharing with me her photocopies of the two novels published in the nineteenth century. Incidentally in *Women Writing in India* the name of the author is spelt Sattianadan, while in the novels it is spelt as Satthianadhan. I have used the spelling as used in the novel. The page numbers refer to the early editions.

3. These details of Satthianadhan's life are taken from the Appendix to the 1895 edition of *Saguna* which contains the tributes paid to the author in a memorial meeting held in Madras after her death.

4. After the first draft of this paper was written, Oxford University Press has reprinted both *Saguna* and *Kamala* in 1998. These new editions do not have the testimonials and other appendages to the novels.

5. Bankimchandra Chatterjee, *Bankim Rachanabali*, vol. I (Calcutta: Sahitya Sansad, 9th edition, 1980), p. 123, my translation.

6. Many early autobiographies by Indian women refer to the hostility of the family to a woman's attempt to read and write, e.g. *Amar Jiban* (Bangla) by Rasasundari Debi (1810–??), *Atmakatha* (Bangla) by Saradasundari Debi (1819–1907), *Amcha Ayushyatil Kahi Athawane* (Marathi) by Ramabai Ranade (1862–1924). Uma Chakravarti writes about the failure of Anant Shastri Dongre (father of Pandita Ramabai Saraswati) to teach Sanskrit to his first wife because of the strong disapproval of the extended family (*Rewriting History: The Life and Times of Pandita Ramabai*, New Delhi: Kali for Women, 1998, p. 303).

7. Chandani Lokuge, 'The Cross-cultural Experience of a Pioneer Indian Woman Writer of English Fiction', in *From Commonwealth to Post-colonial*, ed. Anne Rutherford (Sydney: Dangaroo Press, 1992), pp. 102–16.

8. Raja Rao, Foreword to *Kanthapura* (London: George Allen and Unwin, 1938).

9. Lata Mani, 'The Female Subject, the Colonial Gaze: Reading Eyewitness Accounts of Widow Burning', *Interrogating Modernity*, eds. Tejaswini Niranjana, P. Sudhir and Vivek Dhareshwar (Calcutta: Seagull Books, 1993), p. 265.

10. Meenakshi Mukherjee, *Realism and Reality: The Novel and Society in India* (Delhi: Oxford University Press, 1995), ch. four; 'Women in the New Genre', pp. 68–100.

11. Pandita Ramabai, *A Testimony of Our Inexhaustible Treasure*, first published 1907 (Pune: Pandita Ramabai Mukti Mission, 1992), p. 11.

12. Lakshmibai Tilak, *I Follow After: An Autobiography*, translated from Marathi by E. Josephine Inkster, first published in English, 1950 (rpt. Delhi: Oxford University Press, 1998), p. 134.

13. Examples span countries and cultures. To name a few: *Mary, A Fiction* by Mary Wollstonecraft, *Jane Eyre* by Charlotte Bronte, *The Colour Purple* by Alice Walker, *Sunlight on a Broken Column* by Attia Hosain, *Tehri Lakeer* (Urdu) by Ismat Chughtai (in English translation *The Crooked Line*), *Nampally Road* by Meena Alexander, *Anita and Me* by Meera Syal.

14. Susie Tharu and K. Lalita (eds), *Women Writing in India*, vol. I (New York: The Feminist Press, 1991, p. 244; rpt. Delhi: Oxford University Press).

15. Krishna Chaitanya, *A History of Malayalam Literature* (Delhi: Orient Longman, 1971), p. 275.

16. Pandita Ramabai Saraswati, *Women Writing in India*, vol. I, p. 245.

17. Uma Chakravarti, *Rewriting History: The Life and Times of Pandita Ramabai* (New Delhi: Kali for Women, 1998), *passim* and p. 341.

5

Hearing Her Own Voice: Defective Acoustics in Colonial India

Those working with women's texts are as much aware as those engaged in colonial studies that words like 'voice' or 'authenticity' are not innocent signifiers, imbricated as they are with possibilities of insidious complicity with, or co-option by, the prevailing literary culture. In both cases the dominant and the resistant impulses tend to operate simultaneously in constructing the subject, rendering inconclusive any attempt at locating an unsullied or pristine 'voice'. In reading, as I propose to do in this essay, two women poets who lived in colonial India — Toru Dutt (1856–1877) and Sarojini Naidu (1879–1949) — and who chose to write in the language of the rulers, we find that the issues of gender, language, identity and nation get tangled in knots, some of which remain unravelled even in our seemingly emancipatory post-colonial dispensation.

In a recent essay, Simon During has described the mode of post-colonialism as 'the operation of hearing oneself speak', invoking a sentence by Derrida written in another context. Derrida talked of the situation when 'the subject can hear or speak to himself and be affected by the signifiers he produces, without [them] passing through an external detour — the world, the sphere of what is not his own'.[1] In a situation where the referential world the writer inhabits is not quite of her own making, when she lives in a house not built entirely by herself, the possibility of short-circuiting this external detour becomes particularly difficult. This is so when one is a woman or a colonial subject, but when one is both, the enterprise gets further wrought with invisible complications.

Take for example the paradigmatic case of Toru Dutt, born in mid-nineteenth-century Calcutta, the capital of British India; educated at home by a westernized father until she was fifteen, and then sent to France, Italy and England for four years — to allow her to drink directly at the fount of culture. Then she began to write, first hesitantly, translating French poems into English — an attempt that completely erased the dimensions of her local and Bengali existence — and then gradually more confidently, her own personal lyrics, followed by the re-telling of stories and songs she had heard in her mother tongue. The chronology of her negotiation with different cultural codes anticipated a trajectory that would be replicated many times in colonial art and literature. Toru Dutt died in 1877, when she was only twenty-one, but the two volumes of poems written by her (one published after her death)[2] raise for us questions about literary models and cultural identity, individual voice and the allegorical exigencies of nationhood that have not become dated. Her obvious models were the British Romantic poets but the literary environment of Bengal that she grew up in was, in the opinion of a Bengali poet of our time, Alokranjan Dasgupta: 'a strange fusion of the pseudo-epic and the lyric genres.'[3] The influence of printed words, and that of the immediate context in which she lived, must have overlapped in her work. Members of her own family had a talent for making verses in the English language, an unusual activity in a city where Bangla was certainly the language of literary culture, and was also emerging as the language of nationalist discourse.[4] Bilingualism was the norm in the Calcutta where Toru grew up, English being the language of education and administration, Bangla the language of resistance and creativity.

Or take the case of the other celebrated Indian women poet in English, born in Hyderabad in the nineteenth century, two decades after Toru Dutt. Sarojini Naidu, by her own admission, wrote a 1300-line poem in English by the time she was thirteen, imitating 'The Lady of the Lake' even though she did not speak English at home. The language of her parents was Bangla, the man she married spoke Telugu, and the public language of the Hyderabad of the Nizam was Urdu. Technically, she was not born in British India, but in actuality the princely states were not outside the ambit of British influence and English education. Eventually she published three volumes of poetry in English, which were praised in England and noticed in India, poems which continue to be anthologized in India even now, a century after they were written.[5]

The two poets mentioned above are to be seen not only as historical curiosities — wonder-women of nineteenth-century India who actually wrote poems in English and got published in England at a time when very few women in the country had even primary-level access to this foreign language — but also as writers who continue to engage us, despite many sophisticated debunking attempts in the last half century by different schools of literary thought. There was an early period of eulogy and admiration, mainly based on a nationalistic ardour.[6] Subsequently they have been subjected to attacks of different kinds. Modernists find their poems unacceptable for their romantic effusiveness. Nissim Ezekiel regretted Sarojini's 'ill-luck that she wrote at a time when English poetry had touched the rock bottom of sentimentality'.[7] The post-modernists criticized her work for the false and reactive homogenization of a nationalist paradigm that glorified the past in order to counter the negative image of India perpetrated by the colonial rulers, and more recently postcolonial critics have berated Sarojini's poems for submitting too readily to the Orientalist/exotic view of India.[8] The nature of the attacks and the changes in their emphases are in themselves instructive, echoing as they do successive waves of critical temper in the global arena of literary studies. But before we look at the poems written by these two women and the changing climate of reception and canon formation through which they have had to pass, two other issues have to be touched upon — the interlinked dimensions of gender and language in India.

Language and Gender

It is evident that Toru Dutt and Sarojini Naidu were by no means typical examples of nineteenth-century Indian women. A poet rarely ever represents a constituency, but the non-representative status of Dutt and Naidu needs to be specially emphasized because of the extremely privileged position of their families that allowed them education and mobility (both of them visited England while still in their teens) undreamt of by other women of their generation. It is true that women's education was a much discussed agenda of the reformist movements of the nineteenth century, and there were heated debates in the periodicals in Calcutta and Bombay about the nature and scope of the curriculum suitable for women, but the only area of tacit agreement was that the English language need not form a major part of it. Even nationalist intellectuals agreed that men needed English as the medium of higher education, which would for the time being ensure them jobs in government and expose them to the values embedded in western culture — necessary for both the expansion of their own mental horizons and also the possible subversion of the rulers' control through an understanding of the colonial worldview; but there was little doubt that the women could do without this tool.

As in Victorian England, in colonial India too the separation of the domain of culture into two spheres, material and spiritual, ensured that the women should be seen as custodians of the latter — a realm that belonged outside history. Partha Chatterjee has deftly demonstrated how this abstract dichotomy acquired a concrete and spatial dimension in India in relation to closure and confinement: the home as the internal space of culture that must remain inviolate and uncontaminated by the profane activities of the world outside, 'No encroachment by the coloniser must be allowed that inner sanctum. In the world, imitation of, and adaptation to western norms was a necessity; at home they were tantamount to annihilation of one's very identity.'[9] In the discourse pertaining to women's education in nineteenth-century Bangla newspapers and journals, this taboo on English seems to be so generally agreed upon that one finds hardly any direct reference to it. (This essay confines itself to the situation in Bengal because Bangla happens to be the mother tongue of both the poets being discussed, even though Sarojini lived outside this linguistic region. As it is also mine, I have direct access to its archives.) But the intensity with which the English-educated woman (a somewhat imaginary breed) is mocked at in the Bengali farces and satires of the time as unfeminine, promiscuous and unfit for domestic work betrays a deep-seated fear which may have to do with the danger of empowerment or with notions of individualism or romantic love that the English language might inculcate in the women. The widely circulated myth that women who learned English became widows early in life also indicates the anxiety of the society on this account.

The women of the Bengali upper caste had to be protected from two opposite influences — pernicious for different reasons: from the western ideas that might percolate through English, and also from the crude popular culture of women of the lower strata, which, as Sumanta Banerjee has shown, had a robust vigour and a subversive wit of its own, but which was perceived as obscene by both the Indian bourgeois and the British in India.[11] This is not the place to trace the emergence of the Bengali *bhadramahila* in the sequestered space hedged in by the two danger zones, and examine the genteel verse they produced in Bangla, because the focus in this essay is on women who wrote in English. It seems nevertheless necessary to mention the gender dimension of English in India in order to situate these two unusual women, Toru Dutt and Sarojini Naidu, in their historical and cultural space.

As rare examples of early women poets in English, these two tend to be bracketed together in all discourse on Indian English poetry. I would like to argue in this essay that despite seeming parallels in their education and upbringing, Dutt and Naidu were so diametrically different in their aesthetic ideology and concepts of identity — regional or national — that they cannot be tarred by the same brush nor canonized by the same holy water.

Ask Memory:
She Shall Help My Stammering Muse

Toru Dutt's early flowering (two volumes of verse and an incomplete novel in English, one novel in French, critical essays on Henry Derozio and Leconte de Lisle in *Bengal Magazine*, other pieces in a dozen European and Indian journals,[12] all before she was twenty-one), surprising as it seems today, was perhaps not such an unusual phenomenon in the nineteenth century. There are analogues for such precocity in British literature.[13] It seems incredible today that Mary Shelley's nuanced and complex novel *Frankenstein* (1818), which critics do not tire of explicating from different theoretical positions, was written when the author was barely out of her teens. The consumptive brevity of Toru Dutt's life and of that of her two other talented siblings are also reminiscent in more ways than one of the Bronte family.

Toru's first volume was *A Sheaf Gleaned in French Fields* (1876), a 200-page anthology of French verse in English translation (and a few pieces of Heinrich Heine's German poetry translated into English from their French versions), done in collaboration with her elder sister Aru who too subsequently died very young. It was published through the enthusiasm of their father at Saptahik Sambad press in Bhowanipure, Calcutta, very likely at his own expense, and in a fit of naive parental faith was sent off to London for review. The story of how this shabby-looking orange volume was saved from the waste-paper basket in the editorial office of *The Examiner* by the chance intervention of Edmund Gosse is now legend. Like all legends, fact and fiction get blurred here, but it may be worth retelling if only to remind ourselves how little the situation has changed since colonial times. A favourable review in a British journal secures the reputation of an Indian English writer at home even today, but today the generally accepted pre-requisite for being noticed in the metropolitan press is a British or American publisher's imprint. Recently one of the editors of the *Times Literary Supplement*, when he was in India, candidly stated that books published in India rarely get reviewed in his paper because of their poor production quality.[14] Compared with that, Edmund Gosse's comments in 1876 about Toru and Aru Dutt's volume shows more catholicity:

When poetry is as good as this, it does not matter whether Rouvryre prints it upon Whatman paper or whether it steals to light in blurred type from some press in Bhowanipure.[15]

Toru's second and posthumous volume of poems, whose misleading orientalist title *Ancient Ballads and Legends of Hindustan* (1882) has put off many young Indian readers of the present generation, was published by the respected firm Messrs. Kegan Paul in London, perhaps at the initiative of Edmund Gosse, who wrote the Introduction. Kegan Paul had also reprinted Toru's first volume in 1880.

After a four-year sojourn abroad, the Dutt family came back to stay in the Bagmaree garden house near Calcutta, laden not only with memories of England but with thirteen birds which Aru brought from there (the linnet, the goldfinch and the canary died in the tropical heat), and a packing case 'full of bulbs, roots and seeds from England' ('I hope Mamma will succeed in her attempt to introduce English plants in India', wrote Toru to her friend Mary Martin in Cambridge).[16] Two years later, in a sonnet 'A Mon Pere', this literal fact of transplantation was turned into a metaphor by Toru:

> The flowers look loveliest in their native soil
> Amid their kindred branches; plucked, they fade
> And lose the colours Nature on them laid.

The English material garnered so assiduously during her four years of stay abroad did not sustain Toru for very long ('How tarnished have become their tender hues/E'en in the gathering, and how derived their glow') and even the attempts to invoke memory ('Ask Memory. She shall help my stammering Muse') failed to rekindle the spark.

In her own adolescent way Toru continued nevertheless to be fascinated by the theme of transplantation and biculturalism to which her personal experience had awakened her. She published in *Bengal Magazine* critical studies of two poets of mixed heredity — Henry Derozio (of Indo-Portuguese descent) and Leconte de Lisle (a creole born in Mauritius). In her unfinished novel *Bianca* she makes her heroine a black-haired girl of Spanish descent, whose liminal status in England is highlighted in the plot.

In the second volume of poems Toru Dutt moved away from the double ventriloquism of French-to-English translation in order to write narrative poems she had absorbed from her local milieu. With easy metrical facility she retold the stories of Dhruba and Prahlad, Savitri and Sita — an act that has been acclaimed by her early champions as the assertion of cultural nationalism. One of her enthusiastic biographers, Harihar Das, traced the origins of these tales to Sanskrit originals: 'This work was the result of a year's study of Sanskrit with her father after the return of the family from Europe.'[17] But looking at the chronology of her brief life dispassionately, it seems highly unlikely that ten months of Sanskrit study, undertaken somewhat casually ('Papa says as there is no good opportunity to learn German now, we had better take up Sanskrit'[18]) would have given her enough proficiency in the language to translate or adapt from the original. These stories were part of the Bengali ethos in which Toru breathed, her westernized upbringing notwithstanding. Oral re-telling by her mother would easily have made these stories an inextricable part of her early childhood memories — a fact evoked in Toru's poem 'Sita', which poignantly celebrates the warmth and cosy intimacy which provided the context for the re-telling of the sad tale of Sita's exile. Critics of Toru Dutt have either lauded this narrativization of Indian legends as her acceptance of the glory of her own ancient culture, or seen in it a facile submission to an Orientalist agenda, but as far as I know no one has commented on the specific choice of stories from the wide repertoire of oral tales available to her, focusing, as she mostly did, on women, the lower castes, children, and other marginal creatures — an aspect to which I will return at a later stage.

From the Mocking Bird to the Nightingale

For Toru Dutt, looking homewards for material may not have been a conscious poetic agenda. Unlike Sarojini Naidu, born twenty-two years after her, Toru Dutt did not need a British mentor to remind her that it was not enough to be 'correct in grammar' and 'blame-less in sentiment'[19] — one also had to have an individual voice. In a legendary encounter between an Indian bard and a British critic, Edmund Gosse had urged Sarojini Naidu to give up the English robins and skylarks —

... to set her poems firmly among the mountains, the gardens, the temples, *to introduce to us* the vivid population of her own voluptuous and unfamiliar province; in other words, to be a genuine Indian poet of the Deccan, not a clever machine-made imitator of English classics.[20] (emphasis added).

Fortunately for Toru Dutt, no one had offered her such wisdom and she was left on her own to find her own path. Unfortunately for Sarojini, she took Edmund Gosse's advice, and took it literally.

Years later, Edmund Gosse, in writing the Introduction to Sarojini Naidu's second volume of poems, *The Bird of Time* (1912), recalled how he had put down her early verses 'in despair' because they seemed like competent mimicry of Tennyson and Shelley. 'This was but the mocking bird with a vengeance.'[21] Apparently the prescribed transformation into an 'Indian' poet that Sarojini Naidu subsequently achieved had Gosse's approval. The complexity of the language/power nexus that will never let English be a neutral, value-free medium of creative expression in India is highlighted once again in their relationship. The continuing danger inherent in an Indian writer writing in English is that the native English-speaking literary establishment will automatically constitute itself as both audience and arbiter, providing the criteria of acceptance. Even a critic as sympathetic to India as Edmund Gosse (not only did he praise Toru Dutt and encourage Sarojini, he compared the English sonnets of someone called Priyanath Sen with Goethe's English verses),[22] in his advice to the young girl from Hyderabad, used the phrases 'introduce to us' — insisting that Sarojini should write for the people in England about her 'voluptuous and unfamiliar' province, by a curious sleight of syntax transferring his own unfamiliarity to the poet, and not pausing to think why the daily reality of a city called Hyderabad should be more voluptuous to its inhabitants than Bristol or Liverpool would be to those who lived there.

An obedient pupil, Sarojini Naidu thereafter wrote about the weavers, the palanquin bearers, the bangle-sellers of her city, of the beautiful women behind romantic veils, and of Radha's yearning for Krishna, in lilting rhythm and sparkling metre. Whether or not these poems made 'some revelation of the heart of India, some sincere penetrating analysis of native passion of the principles of antique religion' for its British readers, their deliberate exoticizing of the country has today made her position in the Indian literary history rather precarious. In two of the most sophisticated re-readings on Sarojini's poetry done in recent years by Meena Alexander and Susie Tharu, Sarojini is taken to task for writing in a cloying diction. Makarand Paranjape, who has worked extensively on Sarojini Naidu to provide a new perspective, also admits that 'Her indisputable metrical felicity and technical mastery has not prevented some of her poems from sounding like childish jingles.'[23]

Susie Tharu writes:

Her verse echoes the lyric forms of her contemporary fin-de-siecle British poets; the mood is lyrical, passionate, sentimental as the heart compels, though the local colour is Indian ... [T]he definitive taste is British, although the subjects, ostensibly at least, are Indian.

Valid as this stricture is about the formulaic mode of her poems, one should not overlook some of the other ingredients that contribute to its stylization — the tradition of Urdu poetry prevalent in the Hyderabadi literary culture, a mode that revelled in metaphors of bulbuls and roses, the flame and the moth, the hunter's arrow and the doe; or that of Vaishnava love poetry. To categorize Sarojini Naidu's lyrics as western in conception and exotically Indian in content may lead us to a binary trap. Despite her close personal acquaintance with Arthur Symons (to whom she refers in one of her letters as 'the marvellous boy, with passionate nature and fiery eye'[24]), and others of the Rhymers Club, and some obvious traces of Swinburne in her metre and rhythm, the English component of her work did get modified by other poetic conventions — of the Urdu ghazal for example, or the Radha–Krishna lore, subtly modulating her metaphors and tone.

The situation has a curious analogy with what is now being debated by Indian art historians regarding the paintings of Raja Ravi Varma (1848–1906), whose creative career has a chronological overlap with Sarojini Naidu's. Without attempting to compare their value in the respective domains of Indian painting and poetry, it may be argued that both Naidu and Varma exemplify a moment of complex tension in India's aesthetic heritage and colonial ideology. Raja Ravi Varma emerged in Kerala at a point when 'the changing world of court painting in the South merged with new patterns of patronage, professionalism and commercial success in British India'.[25] He eventually became a national figure popular at all levels, and whose iconic female figures subsequently became the prototype of today's calendar art as well as movie and television representations of the figures from epics and mythologies. It is generally known that Varma struggled to teach himself the techniques of European oil painting, but he used his traditional upbringing and culture, as well as his knowledge of Sanskrit and Malayalam literature, to find the themes of his paintings. Almost parallel to Gosse's Orientalist prescription to the young Indian poet Sarojini, we have a general exhortation to Indian painters, as contained in Lord Napier's (the Governor of Madras) speech on 'The Fine Arts of India' delivered in 1871, where he set out the agenda for developing a 'nationalist painting of India'. Napier called on Indian artists trained in European techniques to deploy their modern skills towards exploring the rich pictorial potential the country offered in her colours, costumes, village scenes, religious festivals — and 'most of all in her ancient mythology'.[26]

Without positing any direct or causal link between Napier's

speech and Ravi Varma's project, it may be recalled the Varma's pan-Indian popularity eventually came to be based on his famous mythological paintings of Shakuntala, Damayanti, Arjun–Subhadra, Vishwamitra–Menaka or Shantanu–Matsyagandha — which achieve an easy transition from the 'regional' to the 'national'. Tapati Guha Thakurta has shown in her analysis of the 1893 oil painting titled 'Malabar beauty' how the ethnic Nair qualities and local markers of Kerala are transformed into an abstracted symbol of larger cultural import, identifiable all over the country. This was one of the ten paintings by Varma that were sent to represent India at an international exhibition in Chicago, and the award that acknowledged both the 'ethnographic' and artistic value of these paintings clearly reaffirmed Varma's national reputation.[27]

Sarojini Naidu's work too acquired an overt 'national' ambience that transcended the merely local or regional. Daughter of Bengali brahman parents who had opted for the Brahmo faith, brought up in Nizam's Hyderabad in the atmosphere of Deccani Muslim culture, married to a Telugu-speaking doctor of the Naidu community, her constituency in any case was elusive and non-definable in a country where identities are determined through a complex intertwining of region, mother tongue, religion, caste and sub-caste. She wrote poetry in English — a language that despite not being anchored in any particular region was peculiarly pan-Indian by virtue of being no-one's mother tongue. This was after all the only language that could be understood by the elite and the educated across the length and breadth of the country.

In regional nationalism, as for example, in Bengal or Maharashtra, the use of English might have had a connotation of colonial servility, but in pan-Indian nationalism, an arena into which Sarojini Naidu was being progressively drawn, English had an important role to play. Although Sarojini Naidu virtually renounced poetry as her engagement with the nationalist movement grew, her reputation as a poet, particularly a poet acclaimed in

England, paradoxically became political capital for her new role. The epithet 'The Nightingale of India' given to her by Mahatma Gandhi clung to her public image as well, making her stature quite distinct from that of other political leaders. The aura of a poet (who also used a mellifluous style in her public speech) added a reso- nance to her person even when she had ceased to have any con- nection with poetry. Her being a woman, her being a poet, particularly a poet in the English language, all became useful ingredients in the construction of her public image.

The abruptness with which Sarojini abandoned her literary career seems to confirm the view that she had really invested not much of herself in her poetry. It was merely an exquisite game played with available poetic counters — eclectically gathered from Urdu and Persian *shairi* traditions, vestiges of Sanskrit formalism, as in the evocation of feminine figures — all heavily laden with British Romantic, Victorian and Pre-Raphaelite verse forms and sensibility. Her disclaimers to Arthus Symons — 'I am not a poet really. I have the vision and the desire, but not the voice' or 'I sing as the birds do, and my songs are as ephemeral'[28] — uttered perhaps as the customary rhetoric of feminine self-devaluation, might nevertheless have contained some truth and might explain her subsequent abandonment of poetry.

Languid and Sequestered

An abiding paradox in Sarojini Naidu's career has to do with the oppositional relationship between the attitudes struck in her verse and her public stand in politics. The person who in 1917 led a delegation of Indian women to meet the Minister for India, Edwin Montague, seeking inclusion of women in the impending government reforms, and who in the 1918 Bombay Congress session put forward the proposal of women's right to vote, was not too long before this writing poems romanticizing secluded women in the zenana (see the poem 'Pardah Nashin' in the Appendix). Also, the woman who in 1908 had moved a motion in the Indian National Conference for the rehabilitation of widows, and in 1906 eloquently spoken for women's 'immemorial birth right ... of liberty and life', in a poem written at about the same time empathized with a woman contemplating sati, endorsing the annihilation of individuality at the altar of wifely devotion as the ideal of womanhood.

It may be argued that the poet Sarojini Naidu's implicitly orthodox stand about a woman's passive and sacrificial role may have smoothened the way to her acceptance as a political leader. The temper of Indian nationalism in the early years of the twentieth century was aggressively traditional, the nineteenth-century reformist zeal about the woman question having been replaced by a valorization of ancient Hindu culture.

The reactionary ideology of Sarojini Naidu's ethnic poems is particularly explicit in the much anthologized 'Palanquin Bearers', which of late has been at the receiving end of several kinds of castigations — feminist and Marxist among others. The labour and ardour of the load-bearers, it is alleged, vanish in the tripping rhythm of the lines they are made to utter.[29]

> Lightly, O Lightly, we bear her along
> She sways like a flower in the wind of our song
> She skims like a bird on the foam of a stream
> She floats like a laugh from the lips of a dream
> Gaily, O gaily we glide and we sing
> We bear her along like a pearl on a string.

In a recent reading of the poem Malashri Lal has taken issue with the poet's unwarranted merger of the labouring man's perspective with the poet's own feudal imagination. The poet gives these lowly, male palanquin bearers the vision of the high-born woman inside the carriage, which they cannot, in reality, have. 'The sequestered woman is faceless, except as a romanticized "type" figure who is borne from place to place on the shoulder of working men.'[30] By implication, the woman is a precious cargo; she has been confined so that her value may remain intact, and this value is spatially transferable, subject to male desire or will. Susie Tharu's critique focuses not on the confined woman, but on the men who bear the burden: 'To see them as they are is discomforting, so they are transformed into a romance that will fit the requirement of European taste, but which at the same time absorbs the labour into the quietism of the lilting form.'[31]

It may not be out of place here to mention that the palanquin bearers, at the time when they plied their trade, did sing to a beat as other manual labourers with a repetitive work pattern still do. The Bangla poet Satyendranath Dutta, a near contemporary of Sarojini, wrote a palanquin song which since then has been set to music, and the tune is familiar to almost anyone who knows Bangla. Unlike the soothing melody of Sarojini's poem, Dutta's song has the rough beat of the walk of the palanquin bearers, the initial sprightliness slowing down to weariness at the end, the burden getting heavier as they go along. The nature of the burden is completely ignored in the Bangla poem — the bearers sing of the road and the details of wayside events. Apart from the obvious fact that Sarojini's poem presupposes the elegance and grace of a nawabi lifestyle, eliding the factor of labour that goes into its maintenance, there is the additional difficulty of making barefoot Indian load-bearers, be they from Bengal or Hyderabad — sing in the cadence of Georgian or Edwardian English. It is worth speculating how much Sarojini's choice of language, and consequently of audience, determined her aesthetic and ideological position, poem after poem conjuring up romantic and colourful moments in a resplendent pageantry, intended presumably to 'introduce' readers like Edmund Gosse to a 'voluptuous and unfamiliar' territory.[32]

A Woman and a Child thus Death Confront

The same argument could theoretically apply to Toru Dutt, but a close reading of her poems reveals a different attitude to the material and to her imagined readership. Notwithstanding the title, the poems contained in *Ancient Ballads and Legends of Hindustan* are not especially marked by hoary antiquity. These are familiar stories told to most Bengali children by a mother or a grandmother. Toru Dutt's early advocates put a nationalist cast on this project, waxing eloquent on her knowledge of Sanskrit and her valorization of India's glorious past. The poem 'Sita' (see Appendix) provides a strong argument in favour of the view that Toru Dutt was only narrating the popular Bangla version of the puranic tales that have circulated orally for generations: the stories of Prahlad and Dhruba, of Dasaratha killing Sindhu, of Ekalavya sacrificing his thumb to Dronacharya. The poem 'Sita' is not only about the unhappy queen of the *Ramayana*, it is about the association the story had, for the poet, of a happy childhood before the family began to be ravaged by death. The poem thus acquires a very private celebratory quality, as if the act of re-telling in some way recuperates the wholeness of the past.

The 'Indianness' of the kind projected by Sarojini Naidu in both her poems and her public speeches[33] seems quite unrelated to Toru Dutt's project. In fact one of the long poems in the collection, 'Jogadhya Uma', narrates a specifically Bengali tale, centring upon a pair of white shell-bangles, which are auspicious markers of a woman's married status only in Bengal — with no such ritual significance attached to them in any other part of India. Also, conceiving the goddess Uma or Durga in purely domestic and familial terms (as a married daughter in this case) is an exclusively Bengali practice which Toru Dutt does not subsume in a larger Hindu ethos of Devi-worship. Unlike Sarojini Naidu, or even Ravi Varma, Toru Dutt seems quite innocent of the desirability of a 'national' projection of Indian culture to counter colonial hegemony. Even the orthography of the Indian words used by her remains stubbornly regional — e.g. 'Joystee' for the month of May–June and not *Jaistha*: 'Drona Charjya' rather than Dronacharya, which would be nearer to the Sanskrit spelling, hence acceptable to more readers across the country rather than its local variant.[34]

'Jogadhya Uma' was translated into twelve pages of metrical Bangla verse by Satyendranath Dutta (the poet mentioned earlier in connection with his 'Palkir gaan' — Song of the Palanquin) in the early twentieth century, a version I read as a girl long before I read the English original. I did not realize it was a translated poem until much later, because the language and the ethos seemed to fit each other effortlessly. The point I am trying to make is that employment of a pan-Indian idiom for the purposes of national projection was very far from Toru Dutt's mind, whose India remained centred in Bagmaree and Maniktola Street, in and around Calcutta. Yet those who have extolled Toru Dutt's poetic virtues have never tired of foregrounding her 'Indianness', a virtue that most Indian writers of English tend to get foisted on them — a quality that is hardly even mentioned while discussing Bangla, Marathi or Hindi poetry. Toru, despite her western orientation, remained curiously local in her conflation of India with Bengal.

One of the earliest retrievers of Toru Dutt's reputation, and the person responsible for the inclusion of her poems in Indian school and college curricula — Amarnath Jha, who wrote an Introduction to her reprinted volume in 1941 — hailed her work as 'an exceptional spectacle in the evolution of the new Indian nationhood'. In those fervently nationalist pre-independence days, he felt compelled to add that 'the insular Englishman may consider them as misguided and ill-advised endeavours destined to inevitable failure. But a disinterested critic will assign to them a fairly high rank from the purely literary standpoint'.[35] More than half a century later, all three points in Jha's encomium seem debatable. The deployment of her work in the services of the newly emergent nationhood, the anxiety about what the Englishman might think of her effort, and the naive belief in the supreme category of the 'purely literary' that stands outside history, race or gender, definitely date Amarnath Jha's response, as much as Edmund Gosse's prediction after her death: 'There is sure to be a page for this tragic exotic blossom of song in the history of English literature.'[36]

It is not in the history of English literature but in that of Indian literature that Toru Dutt has found a space, narrow and tentative, hedged between canonization and dismissal by successive generations of critics. What has been overlooked by both is the subtext of resistance that occasionally surfaces in her seemingly acquiescent work. Her unusual poem 'Buttoo', which narrates the Ekalavya episode from the *Mahabharata*, generally interpreted as a parable of devotion and virtue, can equally effectively be read as a comment on caste brutality. Dronacharya, the teacher who initiated the Pandava princes into the arts of weaponry, haughtily refused to accept as his pupil a boy who came from the wrong caste. The boy went away, and making a statue of Dronacharya in the forest, practised archery in front of this substitute guru till he attained perfection. When, by accident, Dronacharya discovered his skills, he demanded as his guru-dakshina (the homage due to a teacher) Buttoo's right thumb, ensuring that his star pupil Arjuna would never have a rival. The last stanza of the poem describes the subsequent action without comment — the seething anger at the hypocrisy and hollowness of Dronacharya's blessing barely contained by the well-crafted verse.

To praise Toru Dutt for upholding the so-called 'Indian tradition' which is predicated upon caste and gender hierarchy seems somewhat anomalous when in an understated way she carries out a running critique of conventional scriptural wisdom — an enterprise made quite remarkable by the fact that most of these poems

were written before she was twenty. Another example is the poem
'The Royal Ascetic and the Hind', where she puts a twist in the
tail of the story of the ascetic king Bharat who is supposed to have
sinned by becoming unduly fond of a young deer, thus deviating
from the ideal of non-attachment. 'Whatever brahmins wise or
monks may hold', the young poet openly challenges their dic-
tum to declare that the king had not sinned through attachment,
he had sinned by renouncing his kingdom. His declaration of
non-attachment could only be redeemed by the bonds of love.

Even her well-known poem 'Savitri' may be read as a narrative
of female agency rather than of sacrifice and wifely submission.
Susie Tharu's well-known essay 'Tracing Savitri's Pedigree', in
which she traces this paradigmatic feminine figure of Indian
culture through Toru Dutt and Sri Aurobindo to Raja Rao, reads
Toru Dutt's Savitri as a reactive construction of a 'free' woman to
counter the negative image projected by the British and to idealize
a pre-colonial golden past of India.[37]

> In those far-off primeval days
> Fair India's daughters were not pent
> In closed zenanas. On her ways
> Savitri at her pleasure went
> Whither she chose.

But the question of 'freedom' gains an added meaning when the
poem is seen in the context of Toru's personal life. Notwithstanding the Dutt family's liberalism, as an upper-class Bengali woman
in the mid-nineteenth century she herself had very little spatial
mobility. While attending the Higher Lectures of Women in
Cambridge she had briefly tasted a kind of freedom she was never
to regain. When her father abruptly decided that they should come
back, it was not an easy transition for the girls. In 1874 Toru wrote
to Mary Martin, one of her Cambridge friends with whom she
kept up a regular correspondence: 'We all want so much to return
to England. We miss the free life we led there; here we can hardly

go out of the limits of our own garden.'[38] These letters give us the only glimpse of the tensions in the young poet's subjective world, shifted as she was from one culture to another and back, not of her own volition. The longing for England and freedom that punctuates the pages of her letters to Mary Martin makes it difficult for us to put her in either the traditionalist, orientalist or nationalist slots that the critics have so far allotted to her.

There is a wishful projection of the ideal state of being in Toru Dutt's 'Savitri': 'So she wandered where she pleased/In boyish freedom': Savitri is unfettered, mobile like a stream, and free to choose her husband. In Toru's re-telling it is a story not of submission, but of agency. Savitri sees Satyavan, falls in love with him, and insists on marrying him (reversing the expected pattern of the puranic love stories) even though she knows he will die in a year. After their marriage it is she who takes charge, shoring up virtue through prayers and penances for future use. It is she who has the knowledge of impending doom, not her husband Satyavan. On the fatal night she takes the initiative of going out with him to the forest, and after his death she wins him back from the greatest adversary of man — Yama, the god of death — through strategic moves. When Satyavan regains his life, Savitri has to lead him home, axe in hand, clearing the bush ahead. Because Savitri and Sita are indelibly etched in the consciousness of the present generation of readers as retrogressive models of Indian womanhood, personifying submission and suffering, Toru Dutt's eponymous poems are read with an expectation that the actual reading of the poems belies. The poem 'Sita' (see Appendix) is not about the epic heroine at all — it is the frame narrative for all of Toru Dutt's re-telling of puranic tales, nostalgically stating them in a personal setting, of childhood, of the mother's voice at bed time, the vicarious tears for the unhappy queen cementing the bonds of the family, an experience poignant for the poet because of the subsequent loneliness.

Conclusion

It would be fruitless to speculate what Toru Dutt's poems would have been like had she chosen to write in her mother tongue. Her family's conversion to Christianity when Toru was six, and the general western orientation of her anglophile father and uncles — many of whom dabbled in English verse — had pre-determined her option. Writing in Bangla, however, might not have automatically guaranteed a different voice or an unproblematic continuation of an anterior pre-colonial poetic tradition. The major Bangla nineteenth-century poets — all of them male — were also swept off their feet by the British Romantic poetry to which their colonial education exposed them.[39] Women's poetry in Bangla did not have the English models in a direct way, and tended to be formulaic — either devotional or elegiac, mourning a death, sometimes of a husband, subjects that fitted in easily with the approved feminine code of conduct. It was only in the unexpected genre of autobiography — unexpected because this literary form was without precedent in Bangla literary tradition — that the women occasionally broke through this rhetoric of piety and acquiescence to articulate unsanctioned sentiments. Perhaps the absence of a tradition in this genre made such deviations from social propriety or moral norms possible.[40]

Toru died too young to write an autobiography. In Sarojini Naidu's career the growing demands of public action left no space for introspection and reflection on her personal life. We have thus only their poems — two volumes in one case and four in the other — for attempting to unravel the recalcitrant strands that make up their voice, tangled differently in each case, in issues of gender, power, language and nation.

In some ways Toru Dutt's ethos remained very Bengali, even though she happened to *write* in English, an act looked upon with some wariness in the Bengal of her time where the colonial language had already been consciously rejected as a language of creativity. In Toru Dutt's case, however, this wariness of her contemporaries must have been tempered by knowledge of the extreme youth of the poet and the romantic aura surrounding a frail, beautiful and talented girl from an aristocratic family, who died young. Her photograph, reproduced on the cover of the Sahitya Akademi monograph in 1968 — flowing long hair, large luminous eyes in an intense face set above the collar of a Victorian dress — to this day contributes to the image of a unique and fragile creature, not easily appropriated in the larger narrative of the nation. In the hyphenated space she occupied, she could re-tell the legends of Sita or Ekalavya and Sindhu, but she infused the verse with the cadence of Wordsworth and Shelly.[41]

Sarojini Naidu, on the other hand, seemed to have been made for the national stage. The circumstances of her birth, linguistic ethos, education and tutelage (first of Edmund Gosse, then of Gokhale and Gandhi) enabled her to bypass any regional identity altogether, to become first an English poet, then the Nightingale of India, and finally a leader in the Indian National Congress. Like her younger contemporary Jawaharlal Nehru, she arrived at nationalism through England and English, in both cases the interim phase in Britain adding to, rather than detracting from, their national status. Sarojini's gender was an additional factor in her favour because by the time she came to the scene the 'nationalist resolution of the women's question' had more of less been achieved,[42] and the traditional and acquiescent ideology of her poetry fitted in with the notion of the acceptable feminine. Unlike Iqbal or Tagore she did not sing of the nation; she hardly wrote any patriotic verse. But her voice had been recognized as that of a woman who was essentially 'Indian', despite the fact that she wrote in English, or perhaps because of it.

Notes

1. Jacques Derrida, *Speech and Phenomena and Other Essays on Husserl's Theory of Signs*, trans. David B. Allison (Evanston, 1973), p. 78; cited by Simon During in 'Post-Colonialism and Globalisation', *Meanjin*, 51/2 (Winter, 1992), p. 339.

2. *A Sheaf Gleaned in French Fields* (Calcutta, 1976; and London, 1880); *Ancient Ballads and Legends of Hindustan*, with an Introduction by Edmund Gosse (London, 1882).

3. Alokranjan Dasgupta, 'The Fragile Exotic Blossom of Songs', *Indian Literature*, IX: 2, p. 9.

4. A volume entitled *The Dutt Family Album* was published in 1870 containing poems by Toru Dutt's father Govin Chunder Dutt, her uncle Hur Chunder Dutt, and cousins Omesh Chunder Dutt and Greece Chunder Dutt.

5. *The Golden Threshold* (with an Introduction by Arthur Symons, London, 1905); *The Bird of Time* (with an Introduction by Edmund Gosse, London, 1912); *The Broken Wing* (New York, 1917).

6. See Amarnath Jha's Introduction to *Ancient Ballads and Legends of Hindustan* (rpt. Allahabad, 1941). K.R. Srinavas Iyengar and C.D. Narasimhaiah have both emphasized the Indianness of these two poets. Even as late as 1977, A.N. Dwivedi, writing a monograph on Toru Dutt (New Delhi: Arnold Heinemann), declared in the Preface 'One great factor for the revival of interest in Toru Dutt is that India is now a sovereign, democratic republic and is asserting her nationhood ... '.

7. Nissim Ezekiel, *Sunday Standard*, 11 February 1962.

8. See Susie Tharu, 'Tracing Savitri's Pedigree', in *Recasting Women: Essays in Colonial History*, ed. Kumkum Sangari and Sudesh Vaid (New Delhi, 1989), pp. 254–68.

9. Partha Chatterjee, 'The Nationalist Resolution of the Woman Question', in *Recasting Women*, p. 239.

10. For example, *Andare Antare*, a book in Bangla by Sambuddha Chakrabarty (Calcutta, 1995), which deals in detail with women's education in nineteenth-century Bengal, does not mention the question of language at all. Even a text published as early as 1841: Prize Essay: Native Female Education, by Rev. KM. Banerjee (Ostell & Lepage, British Library, Calcutta), which argues that the ancient Hindu scriptures never decreed against women's education, does not mention which language is to be the medium of women's education at the present time.

11. Sumanta Banerjee, 'Marginalization of Women's Popular Culture in Nineteenth Century Bengal', in *Recasting Women*, pp. 127–79.

12. Apart from the two volumes of poems (see note 2), there was Toru

Dutt's novel in French, *Le Journal de Mademoiselle D'Arvers*, published in Paris posthumously in 1879, with an introductory memoir by Clarisse Baden. This novel has been subsequently translated twice into Bangla — in 1949 by Rajkumar Mukhopadhyay and in 1958 by Prithwindranath Mukhopadhyay. Toru Dutt also began a novel in English — *Bianca, or the Young Spanish Maiden*, eight chapters of which were serialized in *Bengal Magazine* (January to April 1874). Her essays on Henry Derozio and Leconte de Lisle were also published in *Bengal Magazine* (December 1874). She wrote frequently for *Calcutta Review* and *Bengal Magazine*. Her writings appeared in other journals too, including *Saturday Review* (London) and *La Gazette de France* (Paris). The full list can be found in Appendix IV of *The Life and Letters of Toru Dutt* by Harihar Das (London, 1921).

13. Norma Clarke in a paper titled 'The Girl-Child Poet: A Woman's Tradition', presented at a Conference on Rethinking Women's Poetry, 1730–1930, in July 1995 at Birkbeck College, London (where an early version of this essay was also presented) discussed several other examples of girl-poets in English literature.

14. This was said by Adolph Wood at a Seminar on 'The Role of Critical Reviews', in New Delhi on 27 February 1995.

15. Edmund Gosse, Introduction to *Ancient Ballads and Legends of Hindustan* (London, 1882).

16. Letter to Mary Martin written on 19 December 1873. From Harihar Das, *Life and Letters of Toru Dutt* (London, 1921).

17. Harihar Das, *Life and Letters of Toru Dutt* (London, 1921).

18. Ibid.

19. Edmund Gosse, Introduction to *The Bird of Time*, by Sarojini Naidu (London, 1912).

20. Ibid.

21. Ibid.

22. Alokaranjan Dasgupta, 'The Fragile Exotic Blossom of Songs', p. 8.

23. Susie Tharu, 'Tracing Savitri's Pedigree', p. 261.

24. Quoted by Makarand Paranjape, from Sarojini Naidu's papers in Nehru Memorial Museum and Library, in the *Introduction to Sarojini Naidu: Selected Poetry and Prose* (New Delhi, 1993).

25. Tapati Guha Thakurta, 'Visualising the Nation', *Journal of Arts and Ideas*, no. 27–8 (March 1995).

26. Quoted by Guha Thakurta, ibid.

27. Guha Thakurta points out that this was the same occasion when Swami Vivekananda gave his famous lecture in Chicago. Around this time Sarojini Naidu was in England, attending lectures in Cambridge and forging friendships with Arthur Symons and other members of the Rhymer's Club.

28. Quoted in Arthur Symons' Introduction to *The Golden Threshold*.

29. Makarand Paranjape, Introduction to *Sarojini Naidu*, p. 14.

30. Malashri Lal, *The Law of the Threshold: Women Writers in Indian English* (Shimla, 1993).

31. Susie Tharu, 'Tracing Savitri's Pedigree', p. 262.

32. Amarnath Jha, Introduction to the 1941 edition of *Ancient Ballads*.

33. Sarojini Naidu in a speech in Hyderabad in 1931 exhorted the students to rise above their linguistic, religious, regional and caste identities to become Indian.

34. Toru Dutt's orthography is indeed a fascinating puzzle at times. Dhruva's father's name in the poem 'Dhruva' is inexplicably spelt Uttanpado, Bhisma in the poem 'Buttoo' is spelt Wismo, Prahlad's brother Anuhrad becomes Onoohrad. A man in the poem 'Prahlad' is given the proper name Sonda Marco, which is probably a version of a colloquial Bengali sobriquet for a strong man (*shonda marka*). Shastras is spelt *Shaster*.

35. Amarnath Jha, Introduction to the 1941 edition of *Ancient Ballads*.

36. Edmund Gosse, Introduction to *Ancient Ballads and Legends of Hindustan*.

37. Susie Tharu, 'Tracing Savitri's Pedigree', p. 260.

38. Quoted by Malashri Lal, *The Law of the Theshold*, p. 43.

39. There are the celebrated cases of two major Bengali writers of the nineteenth century — Michael Madhusudan Dutt and Bankimchandra Chatterjee, both of whom began their literary careers in English, but later shifted to Bangla. Toru Dutt's cousin Romesh Chandra Dutt, who had the same Anglicized background as Toru, made a conscious decision to write his novels in Bangla while he continued to write discursive prose in English.

40. On early women's autobiographies in Bangla, see my paper 'The Unperceived Self: A Study of Five Nineteenth-Century Autobiographies', *Socialisation, Education and Women*, ed. Karuna Chanana (Delhi, 1988), pp. 249–72. Also Malavika Karlekar, *Voices From Within: Early Personal Narratives of Bengali Women* (Delhi, 1991).

41. Notice for example how the rhythm of the second stanza of her poem 'Sindhu' recalls a famous Lucy poem:

> No friends had they, no help or stay
> Except an only boy,
> A bright-eyed child, his laughter gay
> Their leaf-hut filled with joy.

42. Sarojini Naidu's relationship to the Indian languages is not easy to determine. Since her parents were both Bengalis, it would have been natural to assume that she spoke Bangla at home even though they lived outside

Bengal. But her letter to Arthur Symons (quoted by him in the Introduction to *The Golden Threshold*, 1909) describes an incident at the age of nine when she was confined to a room by her father for refusing to speak English: 'I came out of it a full blown linguist. I have never spoken any other language to him or to my mother, who always speaks to me in Hindustani.' Does that mean her mother spoke to her in Hindustani but Sarojini replied in English? It is not clear. Sarojini Naidu's biographer Padmini Sen Gupta claims that she could write Urdu fluently, but she never chose to write poetry in that language. Mulk Raj Anand on the other hand categorically states that she did not read Urdu but loved to hear it spoken ('Conversation with Sarojini Naidu', *Perspectives on Sarojini Naidu*, ed. K.K. Sharma (Ghaziabad, 1989).

APPENDIX

Toru Dutt (1856–77)

Sita

Three happy children in a darkened room!
What do they gaze on with wide-open eyes?
A dense, dense forest, where no sunbeam pries,
And in its centre a cleared spot — There bloom
Gigantic flowers on creepers that embrace
Tall trees; there, in a quiet lucid lake
The white swans glide; there, 'whirring from the brake',
the peacock springs; there, herds of wild deer race;
There, patches gleam with yellow waving grain;
There, blue smoke from strange altars rises light,
There dwells in peace the poet-anchorite.
But who is this fair lady? Not in vain
She weeps — for lo! At every tear she sheds
Tears from three pairs of young eyes fall amain,
And bowed in sorrow are the three young heads.

It is an old, old story, and the lay
Which has evoked sad Sita from the past
Is by a mother sung ... This hushed at last
And melts the picture from their sight away,
Yet shall they dream of it until the day!

When shall those children by their mother's side
Gather, ah me! As erst at evetide?

Sarojini Naidu (1879–1949)

The Pardah Nashin

Her life is a revolving dream
of languid and sequestered ease;
Her girdles and her fillets gleam
like changing fires on sunset seas;
Her raiment is like morning mist,
shot opal, gold and amethyst.

From thieving light of eyes impure
From coveting sun or wind's caress,
Her days are guarded and secure
Behind her carven lattices,
Like jewels in a turbaned crest
Like secrets in a lover's breast.

But though no hand unsanctioned dares
Unveil the mysteries of her grace,
Time lifts the curtain unawares
And sorrow looks into her face ...
Who shall prevent the subtle years,
Or shield a woman's eyes from tears?

6

'We Say Desh':
The Other Nirad Babu

The golden jubilee of India's independence and the centenary of Nirad C. Chaudhuri's birth nearly coincided in 1997–8, creating an occasion to reflect on the once unknown and now eminent Indian's conflictual relationship with the country of his birth. The twin themes that run through all of Chaudhuri's books — barring the two on Max Mueller and Clive — are himself and India, sometimes himself as an Indian, at other times India as defined by his own life. He has written his autobiography over and over for fifty years — in *The Autobiography of an Unknown Indian* (1959), *A Passage to England* (1959), and *Thy Hand, Great Anarch* (1987), and less obviously in most of his other books.

In this compulsive autobiographical impulse, if not in any other respect, two of the most incisive and perspicacious prose writers of our time — V.S. Naipaul and Nirad Chaudhuri — are comparable. Naipaul's life too has been narrated many times — through fiction (*A House for Mr Biswas*), through travelogue (*The Middle Passage, Finding the Centre*) and through a book that blurs the boundaries of genres (*The Enigma of Arrival*). Twice removed form his ancestral origin, and not rooted to any geographical space in particular, Naipaul is not interested in defining a nation, which is Chaudhuri's obsession, but they do have a few other parallels.

Both are profoundly critical of most societies they have come in touch with; both have a predilection for generalizing from isolated personal experiences; both share an impatience with Gandhian thought; and both are moralists by Chaudhuri's definition. I refer to a maxim Nirad Chaudhuri formulated in his twenties and re-iterated when he was nearly ninety, which differentiates between a misanthrope and a moralist thus: 'A misanthrope despairs of himself as well as his fellowmen; a moralist despairs of his fellow-men only' (*Thy Hand, Great Anarch*, p. 130). Neither Chaudhuri nor Naipaul mind the frequent repetitions and overlaps of material in their books. But Nirad Babu has an advantage over Sir Vidia — I do not mean the obvious one of age — of being able to repeat himself in two languages, and also contradicting himself twice over. He has two literary careers in English and Bangla which he has tried to keep separate.

More than a decade ago in my one and only encounter with this legendary man in Oxford, I was reprimanded by him for the im-purity of my language, because a single English word had slipped into my conversation with him in Bangla. Having always been in great awe of his erudition, and apprehensive of his famous eccen-tricities, I would never have had the temerity to initiate a con-versation with Nirad C. Chaudhuri without being prodded by someone else. This push came from my friend Alistair Niven who was incredulous that in spite of being a Bangla-speaking Indian I had never met this monument of unageing intellect. Alistair and I were together in London for a jury meeting of some literary award, and he insisted that I make a special pilgrimage to Oxford to fill this unseemly lacuna in my life by doing a proper *darshan*. 'But what shall I say to him?' I was diffident, reluctant to treat a human being as if he was the Taj Mahal or the Statue of Liberty. 'There is no need for you to say anything. He will do the talking', Alistair egged me on, and, when he discovered that I was in any case going to Oxford that weekend to meet a friend, there was no holding him back. Next morning he called to inform me that he had already told Mr Chaudhuri about my desire to meet him.

This was 1989, long past the days of my youthful enthusiasm when I might have ardently 'desired' to meet a writer. By now I was quite content to read a writer and not to have to make his acquaintance. But there being no decent way of backing out any more, I called the number Alistair had given me. Nirad Babu picked up the phone himself. I mentioned my name and began very hesitantly in Bangla — 'You don't know me, but ... '. 'I know you. I have met you', he interrupted very firmly. I could not imagine where or how. 'At a conference called "The Eye of the Beholder" organized by the Commonwealth Institute in London in 1982'; he gave me the date and place precisely.

It was quite incredible. Indeed such a conference had been held in the era when we were assaulting European countries with our Festivals, quite a few years before Indian writers in English became our major selling commodity in the global cultural market. So much had changed since then that it all seemed like a long time ago. The conference though small, had turned out to be a lively one and to me the star participant there was young Salman Rushdie, a recent winner of the Booker Prize, sharp and energetic, still relatively untouched by the glare of media attention, quite distant from the controversy that would later change his life. Nobody could have thought then that this vibrant young man would one day turn into a staid literary oracle, pronouncing judgement on Indian books he has never read. But another writer present at the same conference was already doing that. To this day I remember Anita Desai's astounding statement made on this occasion which has since been preserved in cold print — ' ... there is very little fiction written by women in India. The few novels that have been written are for the most part in English'.[1]

The conference was memorable for many other reasons. In response to Raja Rao's philosophical statements about Indian tradition — equated almost wholly with the Brahmanic heritage (for Raja Rao knowing Sanskrit was synonymous with being an Indian) — and Professor C.D. Narasimhaiah's assertion that, despite having components of 'Buddhist, Jain, Parsee, Christian, Sikh and Moghul', Indian culture is 'predominantly Hindu', the younger writers intervened with sprightly combativeness. They pointed out that women and lower castes never had access to Sanskrit and a homogenization of India excluded all minorities. The range of participants included the young and old, famous and not so famous, resident Indians like us and our diasporic cousins. On the one hand there were established names like Mulk Raj Anand, Raja Rao and Anita Desai. On the other there were writers like Arun Kolhatkar, Gieve Patel, Faroukh Dhondy and the perpetually angry Sasthi Brata, not to speak of the irreverent Rushdie. There was a freshness in the debate at that point. The first volume of *Subaltern Studies* had just been published that year and its discourse had still not percolated down to all academic and literary spheres to make the questions of minority and marginality routinely central in conference interventions. The word 'post-colonial' had not yet gained currency and the political visibility of Hindu fundamentalism or the international spread of an organization like Vishva Hindu Parishad were still events in the future. The cut and thrust of opposing viewpoints had not yet congealed into a predictable rhetoric. There was a ring of individually thought-out conviction in the opinions expressed which I had found most stimulating.

The reason I did not think of Nirad C. Chaudhuri in connection with this conference was that he was not present for any of these scintillating dialogues. He came from Oxford for the first session to deliver his inaugural address in the evening and went back the same night. Even though I remembered his lecture vividly, I did not connect it with the conference. It was a separate and spectacular performance where he traced the most unexpected and original connections between the English language and Indian culture with none of the ostrich-like complacency displayed by some Indo-Anglian writers who claimed that a literary culture in India other than in English hardly existed. Even at that time I was aware of Nirad Chaudhuri's double persona — as a writer in English and a writer in Bangla — and had a special admiration for him because of this, though I knew he preferred to keep these identities separate. That evening he had come as a writer in English, armed with several exhibits — three textbooks he had studied in Kishoreganj High School in 1908; a Bangla almanac or *panjika* of 1905 which, apart from prescribing exact dates and moments propitious for performing pujas, eating of pumpkins and co-habiting with one's wife, also provided model letters to be written in English; an Intermediate textbook of Calcutta University with an essay on Xenophon by Alexander Grant, and a painting by Romney showing an infant Shakespeare 'attended by Nature and the Passions' found at one time in Shakespeare-adoring Bengali homes. He made dramatic use of these props to situate in history his own evolving relationship with English culture, keeping us spellbound for an hour. He went back to Oxford the same night, not to return for the rest of the conference. He was well past eighty and it was not expected that he would sit through the entire proceedings. As with most inaugural speeches, his talk was not followed by a question–answer session nor did he have, as far as I recall, any informal interaction with the other participants.

I asked him on the telephone how he could have remembered me because I did not have a chance to speak to him on that occasion. 'I have a habit of noticing women, specially young women', he said impishly. Since we were conversing in Bangla, the words he used were *yuvati ramani*, which have an erotic charge, absent in its bland English equivalent. I was amused. 'In that case you do not really remember me, because I am not a *yuvati ramani*', I said. 'Now that I have crossed eighty all women look *yuvati* to me'; his retort silenced me.

We arranged to meet the next evening. I had suggested five o'clock, but he insisted on four-fifteen. My husband also happened to be in London, and we had both been invited for dinner at the house of our friends Trilokesh and Margaret who lived in Oxford those days. We decided to perform the *darshan* together before going on to their place, even though Trilokesh, when he heard of our plan, warned my husband to keep a very low profile, because Nirad Babu, according to him, had a well-known aversion to tall men, and those above six feet were a special anathema. We never found out if Trilokesh was right, but we did notice that my husband was pointedly offered the lowest chair in the living room by our host, while he sat on a fairly high one, presumably his usual seat. I could sit anywhere I liked. But he was affable and charming to both of us alike and kept us riveted for nearly two hours with his reflections on life and literature. This conversation was in Bangla, unadulterated by a single English word. He took me to task for using the word 'India' inadvertently in one of my brief interjections — 'We do not say India, we say *desh*', he admonished me.

He has proclaimed many times in his writing his intolerance of slip-shod mixing of ingredients in sartorial, gastronomic and language practices. He grew up and lived in an age when hybridity was still a negative word and his standards of purity continue to be high indeed. Even in his most recent book, written in his hundredth year (*Three Horsemen of the New Apocalypse*) he has measured the decline of Bengali culture along the rising popularity graph of *idli-vada* and Chinese food. Another cause for lament is the Bengali's abandonment of the elegant *dhoti-kurta* in favour of 'capricious' and tasteless assortments of clothing items, the final vulgarity being the adoption, almost as national dress, of T-shirts with alien logos.[2] On that December evening of 1989, he welcomed us in a *dhoti* and a brown flannel *kurta* of the kind commonly seen in our childhood, but gone out of use in recent decades. He insisted on bringing in the tea-trolley himself, graciously declining my attempts to help him: 'Guests who have come to our house for the first time are not allowed to do any work.' Mrs Chaudhuri sat with us and participated in the conversation, but her arthritis kept her confined to a wheelchair.

It was so easy to sit back and listen to him that I soon forgot my earlier apprehensions. He particularly warmed to us when he found that we knew very closely his contemporary from Calcutta University — Sudhanshu Kumar Das who retired as a judge of the Supreme Court of India in 1963 — another admirable human being who continued to be interested in books, ideas and people right until his death in 1994 in Delhi. Perhaps that 1898 model of human beings was very special, not repeated since then. Nirad Babu also probed our Patna background and came up with names of people like Rangin Haldar who he knew in his youth. All went well until at one point I opened my mouth a bit too wide and put my foot into it.

In response to his query about how long we were going to be in London, I said perhaps a week or ten days more, because I had to do some reading in the British Museum. 'What do you want to read?', he fixed me with a stare. At that time I was writing a monograph on Jane Austen for the Macmillan Women Writers Series, and had set upon myself the task of reading all the late eighteenth-century best-sellers in England that young Jane might have read herself — books either mentioned or obliquely referred to in her novels. This incensed him. 'You are writing a book on Jane Austen! How well have you read her own novels?', he challenged me. 'Fairly well, I think', I said guardedly, taking courage from the fact that Jane Austen, like E.M. Forster, was one of the few English novelists whose complete works could be read thoroughly even without making it a life-time occupation. Mrs Chaudhuri, who seemed to be an amused observer of her husband's idiosyncracies, at this point exclaimed with a smile directed at me: 'Now you have got yourself into trouble!' I did not know at that time that Jane

Austen was one of Nirad Babu's favourite writers and he read a few pages from her novels almost every night.

What followed was a close interrogation of my textual knowledge of the six Jane Austen novels in which examination, I must confess, I barely managed a 'B' grade. It involved remembering details of Darcy's clothing on specific occasions, knowing the meaning of certain colours of British heraldry, the distance between Hunsford and Longbourne, the number of horses used for drawing different kinds of carriages and the like. The one that completely floored me had to do with the size of Fanny Price's room in the attic in *Mansfield Park*. To this day I cannot figure out how he worked it out. As he explained to me, it had something to do with the space taken up by Fanny's bookshelf which he calculated by locating the original edition of each book mentioned and adding up their dimensions. I was not convinced, because I did not think all the books Fanny read were mentioned in the novel, but discretion seemed the better part of valour. He took pity on me after a while and decided to let me off the hook, promising to send me a piece on Jane Austen he had written for the *Times Literary Supplement*. A few days later in London I did receive the promised piece in a packet along with a pen carefully wrapped in cotton wool which I had left behind in Nirad Babu's house.

That was ten years ago. I have often wondered since then, specially while reading Nirad Babu's Bangla work, whether when he upbraided me about my use of English and asked me to say 'desh' he was really giving me an equivalent of 'India'? Earlier I had carelessly believed that his Bangla writing was an offshoot of his English work, similar in attitude, content and range, if not in style. His use of verbs in their chaste form (*sadhu bhasha*) as against the colloquial form certainly set him apart from Bangla writers of today as being deliberately old-fashioned, and he has never concealed his contempt for the more informal version of the language as it is written now. Since English does not have a similar grammatical marker to set apart old and new usages, he does not stand out from contemporary English writers in so obvious a manner, even though other stylistic features may remind the reader of his vintage. But this is only a superficial difference. I am beginning to believe that his agenda and objectives are fundamentally different when he is writing in English and in Bangla.

Language can play strange tricks with our perceptions and self-images. Who knew it better than Nirad Babu, who had pointed out several anomalous examples of this in the inaugural speech mentioned above.[3] But he seems to have been an unconscious prey to these paradoxes himself. While in his English autobiography in 1951 he had identified himself as an 'Unknown Indian', in a Bangla piece he rejected this identity emphatically. He declared: 'I project myself as a Bengali, never as an Indian. The more recent appellation "Asian" I cannot even dream of using.'[4] He pre-empts possible charges of inconsistency by pleading amnesia in another essay 'Akshamer Kshamata' (The power of the powerless): 'When I write in English I completely forget that I know Bangla; similarly while writing Bangla I do not remember knowing any English.'[5]

Such overstatements are familiar features of his style and need not be taken literally. But English and Bangla do provide him with different perspectives and two target audiences, provoking him to assume contradictory positions. In his recent English book he claims to have 'a complete knowledge of Bengal',[6] but only two years before that in a Bangla essay he had confessed that, after he left Calcutta for Delhi in 1942, he hardly had any contact with Bengal, and 'since 1970 I have been in Oxford, I have not been back even once. Thus I have no direct knowledge of Bengali life.'[7] Such contradictions seem fairly frequent when his works in two different languages are read side by side.

Shri Niradchandra Chaudhuri (in Bangla he always used the complete form) published his first full-length book *Bangali Jibane Ramani* (Women in Bengali Life) in 1968, stating in the Preface: 'At the age of fifty I wrote my first English book; at the age of seventy this is my first in Bangla. I thought it was late for English; I shudder to think how late it is for Bangla.'[8] It was not as if he was writing in Bangla for the first time, because he was part of a literary coterie in Calcutta in his youth, and in 1927–8 served as the editor of the journal *Shanibarer Chithi* (The Saturday Letter), well known for its scathing critical pieces and acerbic wit. Among his closest friends was Bibhutibhusan Banerjee, known outside Bengal mainly as the author of *Pather Panchali*, and Chaudhuri has written about their friendship on several occasions, including in *Thy Hand, Great Anarch*. Later, in 1932, Nirad Babu worked for another well-known Bangla journal *Probashi*. But after he left Calcutta in 1942 he was out of touch for thirty years and returned to Bangla first with long essays in the weekly *Desh* in the mid-sixties, to be followed by this controversial book in 1968, written at the insistence of a literary friend of his youth, Gajendra Kumar Mitra, who had by this time turned publisher.

Bangali Jibane Ramani presented a unique thesis about the role of English literature in the evolution of *kama* (physical desire) into *prem* (romantic love) in nineteenth-century Bengali life. This was a 300-page elaboration of a point he had briefly made in *A Passage to England*:

We in Bengal began to deal with love from a literary end. That is to say it was transferred to Bengali literature from English literature, and then taken over from literature to life. As a result of this double transplantation, the plant remains delicate and a hothouse atmosphere is needed for its survival.[9]

This is an excellent example of his tendency of elevating a particular observation to the status of a general truth. It is not surprising that he should think his autobiographies serve the double purpose of also being cultural histories of India. Whatever he has experienced becomes the truth — often for all Bengalis, sometimes for all Hindus, occasionally for all Indians. Because he responds to life only when it is refracted through the prism of art and literature, he makes a sweeping judgement that all Indians perceive life second-hand. Consider the following pronouncement from *Thy Hand, Great Anarch*:

... indifference to the geographical environment of their life was part of the traditional attitude of all Bengalis. Before they had become conscious of nature by reading English poetry, they did not show any awareness even of the Himalayas, although they had some of the peaks just north of Bengal. (p. 206)

It is ironic that such a stricture should come from one who himself cannot look at nature in India without mentally linking it with something British. Describing in retrospect a walk in his village Kishoreganj during his adolescence, he observes: 'The whole scene was like one of Constable's landscapes' (p. 210) and about watching the sandbanks of the river Padma from a steamer he has the following comment: 'I had just read about Turner's paintings in a book ... The glow of his paintings, visualized by imagination, seemed to be on the wide landscape all around me' (p. 209). He cannot mention even Sabzi Mandi in Delhi without adding that it is like Covent Garden in London (p. 686). Mimicry cannot go further — mimicry not in the Homi Bhabha sense, but in its original dictionary meaning.

But this subordination to a western frame of reference is more common in his English writing than in Bangla. In *Bangali Jibane Ramani* he marshalls an impressive array of evidence to prove his thesis, supporting his argument not only through quotations from Sanskrit and Bangla literary texts (from Bhababhuti, Kalidasa, and Jaidev to Bharatchandra, Chandidas, Bankimchandra and Rabindranath), but from less respectable sources as well: bawdy wedding songs, rustic doggerel, and snippets of women's conversations remembered from his rural childhood, where parts of the body were referred to in a diction that still exists in crude speech but has rarely ever found its way into print. Since the time Nirad Babu mischievously introduced the gross vocabulary of popular culture in a serious discourse on nineteenth-century Bengal, detailed research has been done in this field, particularly by Sumanta Banerjee[10] who demonstrates how this 'low' culture, often associated with women, was a source of embarrassment for the English-educated enlightened Bengali. It has to be said for Nirad Chaudhuri's Bangla writing that he constantly reminds his readers that behind the much-discussed *bhadralok* way of life there was a strong popular culture vibrant in its crude energy.

His peppering learned essays with Bangla equivalents of four-letter words had the desired effect of outraging Bengali readers into writing long irate letters to the editor when some earlier versions of this book appeared in *Desh*. In fact, he remained a controversial writer in Bangla for a long time, a large number of readers strongly taking the rather simplistic position that, as a blind admirer of everything Western, Chaudhuri has made a career out of debunking India, particularly Bengal. Another popular myth that he belittles Rabindranath Tagore does not bear close scrutiny, because his range of reading in Tagore is amazing and his anguish at the blind iconization of the poet by Bengalis who hardly know his work has to be taken seriously. In fact his long essay 'Rabindranather Aparahna' (The Afternoon of Rabindranath) about the loneliness of the poet who received the Nobel Prize is one of his most moving pieces of writing in which he sees this prize as casting a dark shadow of false fame over Rabindranath's true achievement.[11] For many years anything written by Nirad Babu in *Desh* — a journal well-known for its lively correspondence columns — was followed by rejoinders and attacks lasting over months. Of late, however, perhaps in deference to his age, or because or a growing mellowness of his own tone, the controversy seems to have ebbed somewhat.

Not many people know that when he (as well as the century) was in the early thirties, he delivered a public speech in a literary gathering at Calcutta condemning the Bengali attitude of superiority in relation to the rest of India. He argued that the political future of the country lay with Hindi, the language of the majority in India, which possessed dynamism and vibrancy. In the Introduction of *Thy Hand* he recalls: 'By the nineteen-thirties I had fully realised that there was no future for the Bengali people and their culture' (p. xxiv). The first part of the speech was published in the Bangla journal *Probashi*, but the editor Ramananda Chatterjee refused to publish this second part which he thought was too severe a castigation of the Bengalis. Later Chaudhuri changed his position on Hindi too:

... by the time independence came to India, I [had] discovered that speakers of Hindi were in no better predicament than we Bengalis. I even found that they were sunk deeper in decadence, for they were fossilized, while we in Bengal were decomposing (p. xxv).

During his temporary enthusiasm for Hindi he had been deeply influenced by a colleague, Banarasidas Chaturvedi, who worked for the Hindi magazine *Vishal Bharat*. (Ramananda Chatterjee was perhaps the only person ever in India who edited separate journals in three different languages — *Probashi* in Bangla, *Vishal Bharat* in Hindi, and *Modern Review* in English.) Chaturvedi was an erudite man who, according to Chaudhuri, 'spoke and wrote English with elegance' — a compliment he has rarely paid to any other Indian — and was 'something of a specialist on Indians living in British colonies abroad' (p. 333). But later in life when the other Hindi writers he met did not measure up to Chaturvedi's standards, he reverted to his position of Bengali centrality that subsequently expressed itself in his English writing, although in his Bangla writing he has consistently been a critic and a fault-finder of the Bengali people in general.

Much of his controversial status in Bangla is of course of his own seeking. His Bangla corpus, which may be seen as an almost continuous reflection on Bengali life, literature and history, segmented in several books and long essays (one of his books, incidentally, is called *Atmaghati Bangali*, 1988 or The Suicidal Bengali), is also a ceaseless introspection of his own love–hate relationship with his origins, and by varying the tropes in describing the tension he brings to bear new perspectives on the topic. At one point he thinks of Bengal as a stagnant lagoon and decides to abandon it to sail on the open ocean. 'A rupture happened between me and life and society in Bengal which continues even today. I am moving and will continue to move. They are static.' [12] At another place he uses the Tagore story 'Streer Patra' (Letter from a Wife; written in 1914) as a metaphor for his feelings towards Bengal. When Mrinal, the rebellious second daughter-in-law of a joint family in Calcutta escapes from the claustrophobic household to come face-to-face with the sky and the sea, she realizes how confined her earlier life had been. Referring to this Nirad Chaudhuri writes:

Like Mrinal I can now say, "Where are your walls of masonry now, where are the barbed wire fences made up of rules and prohibitions? Your insults and humiliations cannot keep me imprisoned any more ... You had kept me concealed in the gloom of your mindless routine. Only after coming outside I can see myself in my full glory."[13]

Elsewhere he compares his creative freedom after coming out of Bengal with the dance of Kipling's Kaa after his change of skin (*The Jungle Book*), which the monkeys watched with hypnotized fascination. 'The educated Bengali has not been able to take his eyes off my dancing since 1951, and will not be able to, as long as I am alive.'[14]

Yet he feels the need to carry on a dialogue with the people he has rejected, and keeps providing various justification for renewing his career in Bangla so late in life.

Bengalis look at their own people writing in English in the same way they respond to wild animals performing in a circus — not as a natural act but as tricks learnt through rigorous discipline. The more intricate the act the more they applaud; this writing may appeal to their head, but it does not touch the heart.[15]

Writing in Bangla, evidently, is the only way to touch their heart. At another place he declares that he has no desire to be known as a writer in Bangla: 'The intention is not to achieve literary fame, but merely to carry on a conversation with the Bengali people about their history and religion. As long as they listen to me I do not care if I am recognized as a writer.'[16] In yet another place he confesses:

I have realized I cannot reach the educated Bengalis today through my English writing. Firstly, they have lost the habit of reading English. They do not read easily and therefore they do not enjoy what they read. Secondly, most Bengali readers no longer have the ability to appreciate the kind of English that British publishers find acceptable. Perhaps they understand half the meaning, but the resonance and significance of the other half is lost to them. The English that is current in England is thus only partially accessible to the Bengali. Then why write in English for them? In the present reduced state of the Bengali people, if anyone has anything to say to them, it should be conveyed in a language they can comprehend.[17]

True to his quirky temperament, after having made these contradictory statements — one appealing to the heart, the other arrogant and condescending — he went on to write books and essays that hardly need these declarations. In a disarming autobiographical piece — perhaps meant to be in the mode of Rousseau or St Augustine — he confesses his own meanness and vulnerability, his profligacy, his neglect of work, his inordinate delight at having received a generous dowry, his self-indulgence and vanity. He describes in an amusing manner how he never paid for the dentures he got made before getting married and how on his wedding night he had the presumption to ask his bride if she could spell Beethoven. But at the end of this candid and human story he

suddenly remembers his agenda and holds forth on how the entire
narrative is written for the benefit of the defeated Bengali people
so that they too can learn how to succeed in life.

Shri Niradchandra Chaudhuri sought to bid farewell to his
second career in 1996 by writing an essay whose title can be translated as 'My Last Words to the Bengali People'.[18] The year after,
he wrote another piece titled 'A Post-script to My Last Words'.
He never lived to write a 'Post post-script' to clarify at least one
slippage of concepts between his two languages. He taught me to
say *desh* for homeland, which is presumably India when he is
writing in English. Why was it necessary to narrow it down to a
non-existent Bengal whenever he took up the crusade in his
mother tongue?

[All English translations from Nirad Chaudhuri's Bangla writing quoted here
are by me.]

Notes

1. Anita Desai, 'Indian Women Writers', in *The Eye of the Beholder: Indian Writing in English* (London, 1983), p. 54.

2. Quoted from the extract in *India Today* (28 July 1997) from *The Three Horsemen of the New Apocalypse*, p. 90.

3. For example, he mentioned a line in a model letter in English published in a 1905 almanac where an Indian father is supposed to be writing to his son: 'Your mother, like myself feels aggrieved that you have asked for an additional allowance.' Nirad Chaudhuri's comment is, 'A Hindu would not write "your mother and I", but "I and your mother". We could not write in English without changing mentally.' *The Eye of the Beholder*, p. 10.

4. 'Bangalir Kacche Aamar Shesh Katha', *Desh* (sharadiya), 1402, p. 137.

5. 'Akshamer Kshamata', *Desh* (sharadiya), 1400, p. 55.

6. *India Today*, 28 July 1997, p. 90.

7. 'Bangalir Kacche Aamar Shesh Katha', *Desh* (sharadiya), 1402, p. 132.

8. Preface to *Bangali Jibane Ramani* (Calcutta, 1968), p. 10.

9. *A Passage to England* (London, 1959), pp. 115–16.

10. 'Marginalisation of Women's Popular Culture in Nineteenth Century

Bengal', in *Recasting Women*, ed. Kumkum Sangari and Sudesh Vaid (New Delhi, 1989).

11. 'Rabindranather Aparahna', *Desh* (sharadiya), 1398, p. 158
12. 'Akshamer Kshamata', p. 63.
13. 'Bangalir Kacche Aamar Shesh Katha', *Desh* (sharadiya), 1402, p. 134.
14. Ibid.
15. 'Akshamer Kshamata', *Desh* (sharadiya), 1400, p. 55.
16. Preface to *Bengali Jibane Ramani*, p. 15.
17. Ibid, p. 14.
18. 'Bangalir Kacche Aamar Shesh Katha', *Desh* (sharadiya), 1402.

7

Maps and Mirrors:
Co-ordinates of Meaning in
The Shadow Lines

... Kokovoko is an island far away to the West and
South. It is not down in any map; true places never
are.

Melville

... the baffling mirror ... the implied associations ...
which the native illusionist can magically use to transcend the heritage in his own way.

Nabokov

If maps attempt to chart the earth's surface precisely, mirrors deal
with illusory space. The recurrence of these two tropes in
Amitav Ghosh's *The Shadow Lines* (1988) alerts us to the shifting
reaches of meaning in a novel where the simultaneity of precision
and illusion transforms our perceptions of both space and time.
Just as cartography is the science of codifying space, history is the
discipline of narrativizing time. The public chronicles of nations
are interrogated in this novel by highlighting on the one hand the

reality of the fictions people create around their lives ('stories are
there are to live in, it was just a question of which one you chose')
and on the other by recording the verifiable and graphic details of
individual memories that do not necessarily tally with the received
version of history. Similarly a realignment of the sense of geography happens through an acknowledgement of the subjective space
that all human beings inhabit (a 'secret map of the world of which
only I knew the keys and co-ordinates') and also by plotting the
different points of the globe on the accurately measured pages of
the Bartholomew Atlas, 'within the tidy ordering of Euclidian
space'.

This Bartholomew's Atlas occupies a distinct and palpable space
in the novel. A brand new copy of the atlas which was given to
nine-year-old Tridib as a birthday gift in a bomb-devastated London reappears forty years later in a tattered form at the bottom of
a bookshelf in Delhi. The details of the story of Tridib's stay with
the Prices at Lymington Road during the Second World War are
so indelibly etched on the young narrator's mind that, thirty years
later, as a boy in Calcutta in the early sixties he can vividly re-live
his uncle Tridib's experiences, conjuring up 'the ghost of the
nine-year-old Tridib sitting on a camp bed ... his small face intent,
listening to the bombs'. The first of the many mirror images in the
novel appears on the opening page where the unnamed narrator
deliberately superimposes the child Tridib's identity on his own.
Tridib went to England when he was eight: 'I have come to believe
that I was eight too when Tridib first talked to me about this
journey ... I had decided that he looked like me.'

Tridib the mentor, on whom the child projected his self,
pointed out places in the Bartholomew's Atlas while telling him
stories —'Tridib had given me worlds to travel in and he had given
me eyes to see them with' — so that long before he actually moved
out of Calcutta, his world had expanded to include many parts of
the globe through hearing and reading about these places. Cairo,

Madrid, Cuzco or Colombo, names that his globe-trotting cousin Ila mentioned casually, were for the narrator 'a set of magical talismans' to be invested with reality through precise imagination in the way Tridib had taught him, though he knew he could never replicate the same feat:

And still I knew that the sights Tridib saw in his imagination were infinitely more detailed, more precise than anything I would ever see.

Tridib had told him of the desire that can carry one beyond 'the limits of one's mind to other places, and even, if one was lucky, to places where there was no border between oneself and one's image in the mirror'. Distance in *The Shadow Lines* is thus perceived as a challenge to be overcome through the use of imagination and desire until space gets dissolved. One of the many intricate patterns that weaves the novel together is the coalescing of time and space in a seamless continuity, memory and imagination endowing remembered places and recounted lives with solidity. But for a person locked in the present — like Ila — maps and memory are equally irrelevant; all the cities she had lived in 'went past her in an illusory whirl of movement, like those studio screens in old films which flash past the windows of speeding cars'.

Names of unknown places form the litany of the narrator's childhood not only through the lore brought back by the foreign service branch of the family — Bratislava, Konakry, Sophiya — but also through twice-removed reports like the life story of the Englishman Tresawsen who is said to have travelled in Malaysia, Fiji, Bolivia, the Guinea coast and Ceylon before coming to India, or through the encyclopaedic repertoire of Tridib who could hold forth on the Mesopotamian Stalae and East European Jazz as easily as on the archaeological sites associated with the Sena dynasty of Bengal. The child narrator is told that in the Raibajar house near Calcutta, the rain forests are imported from Brazil and Congo. This global gamut may at first appear to be an unusual backdrop for the story of an ordinary Bengali boy who is taught from childhood how to hang on to the precarious survival slope of middle-class gentility by doing well in examinations. Paradoxically though, this sub-text of geographical inclusiveness helps to situate the narrator very firmly in his specific cultural milieu.

Cartographic imagination has characterized an aspect of Bengali sensibility in ways that have yet to be analysed. Whether as a result of a relatively early exposure to colonial education or as a reaction to it, real journeys within the country and imagined travels to faraway places outside national boundaries have always fascinated the Bengali middle class. Publishers claim that the sale of travel books in Bangla ranks second only to that of religious books, and even a casual tourist would confirm that Bengalis outnumber travellers from any other single region of India. They do not always come from social classes where holidays are an easily affordable luxury.

Children's books in Bangla, at least until a few decades ago, used to abound in stories about African forests, Arab deserts and glaciers that challenge human ingenuity and endurance. Adult literature also often dwelt on the attraction of unknown spaces. Bibhutibhushan Banerjee or Jibanananda Das had never crossed the borders of India, yet they wrote of the groves of cinnamon in equatorial forests and prairies across vast continents. Opu, the hero of Banerjee's two-part novel (*Pather Panchali*, 1929 and *Aparajito*, 1931) could, while growing up in the village Nishchindipur in Bengal, imaginatively evoke the Mediterranean Sea and the distant lands of South America and Japan. As a young man in Calcutta he looked at the ships at anchor in the Hooghli with desire and longing. At the end of the second volume he actually leaves the country from the port of Calcutta on a ship bound for South America — perhaps the most distant point Bengali imagination could traverse in 1931 when the novel was written, and as far away from England as possible on the globe. This kind of wishful ending can be seen either as a romanticization of geography or an implicit bid to escape the colonial grid on which Europe mediates the world in the rhetoric of binariness.

But these travels do not signify any dislocation, because, as in *The Shadow Lines* so in Banerjee's novels, time and space are dimensions of an individual's desire in which the actual and the imagined coexist harmoniously. In his childhood Opu had read of a sunken ship off the coast of Porto Plata. When he embarks on his actual voyage, he connects it with the recovery of the precisely invented treasures of this fabled ship that he has carried in his mind for years. Childhood fancy is collapsed into a supposedly real adult experience, not very unlike the blurring of temporality and levels of reality in *The Shadow Lines*.

A paradigmatic fictional figure, Tridib very easily fits into this inclusive narrative tradition that privileges that traveller/imaginist, reminding the Bengali reader occasionally of the Ghana-da stories by Premendra Mitra, and slightly more peripherally of the Pheluda stories by Satyajit Ray, in both of which a boy is held spellbound by a somewhat older person's encyclopaedic knowledge of other lands and other civilizations. The newest incarnation of this prototype is the eponymous uncle in the last Ray film, *Agantuk*, whose visits to far away places in the globe and knowledge about various tribes invest him with an aura of depth and authenticity that the people caught up in the quotidian details of daily routine lack. And this does not necessarily alienate him from his home, the centre from which the arcs of travel radiate. Neither 'alienation' not 'marginality' — terms made current by modernism and postmodernism respectively — can appropriately describe this phenomenon.

The tracing of this uneven literary lineage is done here not so much to claim that *The Shadow Lines* might as well be a Bangla novel written in English, but to emphasize the concreteness of the essential and emotional milieu in which Tridib and his reflected

image — the unnamed narrator — are situated. Despite his ano-
nymity, the narrator of *The Shadow Lines* is a firmly placed character. The precise class location of his family — Bengali bhadralok,
starting at the lower edge of the spectrum and ascending to its
higher reaches in one generation, with family connections above
as well as below its own station — is minutely recorded. The spatial
movement, from a flat in Gole Park to a house in Southern Avenue
with the 'conversation-loving stretch' of Gariahat Road occupying
a central space, charts his Calcutta moorings precisely. The relent-
less education compulsions of this class and the tension of conflicting values between its dominant and deviant members are evoked
with as much telling detail as the frequent shifts of locale and the
sequence of the public events that frame his life. The documentary
accuracy might even lead one to believe that the primary agenda
of the novelist is verisimilitude, his basic mode of representation
realism. The spatial imagination and the passion for entering other
lives that the narrator imbibes from Tridib enables him to be
mimetically situated in a special cultural milieu. Yet by the end of
the novel certain major shifts have taken place that destabilize the
simple equation between events and their written report, under-
cutting the basis of formal realism in which the credibility of the
representation is predicated upon a firm knowledge of what has
happened. An indeterminacy about this knowledge invalidates
realism as a narrative mode in *The Shadow Lines*.

Knowing and not knowing are so intricately linked in this novel
that their interaction seems to hold the key to its meaning. We
know not only the names of the places the narrator describes, but
often their exact addresses also (the Prices lived in 44 Lymington
Road in West Hampstead; the old house in Dhaka was 1/31
Jindabahar Lane) and the brand names of objects are meticulously
mentioned (Rennie's digestive tablet, Lyon's assorted toffees; the
watch is Omega, cars are Studebakers, Mercedes of Citroens;
Nick's shirt is from Turnbull and Asser, his Jacket from Armani).

But amidst this welter of minutiae there is one blank space deliberately left so. We never get to know the narrator's name, nor can we visualize what he looks like except through occasional glimpses of the various other persons whose mirror image he is supposed to be; Ila ('She and I were so much alike that I could have been her twin') or Nick ('a spectral presence beside me in my looking glass').

The transparency of the unnamed and undescribed narrator lets different persons, events, places luminously enter his story, and find new configuration there; or, altering the metaphor, it is possible to see the narrator's consciousness as a porous space that absorbs other lives and other experiences until their colours leak into each other to reveal a pattern. Whichever metaphor is chosen, the narrator remains not only the large lucid reflector but also the agentive site where random shards of memory are realigned towards some measure of coherence.

Maps in this novel are not confined to the atlas; floor plans drawn in the dust by children playing Houses provide a clue to the past and future reality; long before the narrator left home he knew the A to Z map of London so well — particularly page 43, square 2F, where the Price house was located — that the first time he came to London he could lead Nick and Ila confidently along the roads of West Hampstead as if he had lived there himself. Every representation of space in the novel — rooms, houses, neighbourhoods, city, country, borders and maps — assumes a semiotic signification over and above the literal context. The underground room in the Raibajar house with the shrouded furniture and the large dining table recurs in the novel as an actual location and a remembered site holding a clue to Ila's shabby secret — as a child when she was abandoned by Nick and as an adult when she was betrayed by him. Just as the Prices were first mentioned in a story made up by Tridib, and eventually turn out to be real people, Nick too is first mentioned by Ila in a game of make-believe played under a vast dining table, and then gets transformed into the narrator's adversary and mirror image. 'I would look back into the glass, and there he would be, growing, always a head taller than me.' Incidentally, when he actually met Nick in London as an adult his height and width turned out to be illusory, only a trick of light on the railway platform, showing him to be exactly his own size, reinforcing the mirror image all over again. It is again in this basement that the imagined doll Magda grows into an image of Ila — a real girl who goes to school in London and re-enacts Ila's experience of racial harassment; but it is a mirror reflection that also transforms — her hair turns golden and her eyes deep blue, revealing racial anxieties belied by Ila's façade of uncaring confidence.

By a sleight of vision this underground room turns into the cellar of the Price house in London where two of the most poignant moments in the novel are placed, and through the play of memory the different temporal segments are fused in an oneiric image of wholeness:

Those empty corners filled up with remembered forms, with the ghosts who had been handed down to me by time; those of the nine-year old Tridib ... the ghost of the eight-year old Ila, sitting with me under that vast table in Raibajar, they were all around me, we were together at last, not ghosts at all; the ghostliness was merely the absence of time and distances — for that is all that a ghost is, a presence displaced in time.

Time in this novel can be illusory and concrete at the same time, and likewise space can be fluid even when held solidly within the concrete scaffolding of a house or confined within the firm outlines etched as national boundaries on a map. Houses — whether they are in Brick Lane, Ballygunge Place or Dhanmundi — are each encased in different sets of vividly evoked specificities, baffling the narrator with 'the mystery of difference'. The sloping roof of the Colombo house, which he has not seen but has heard being described, is not just an architectural detail, but a new way of life to be imagined with effort by a boy who has grown up in a flat-roof `culture. 'What would it be like to live under a sloping room — no place to fly kites, nowhere to hide when one wanted to sulk, nowhere to shout across to one's friends.' It is on the roof, under the shade of the rusty water tanks that he would slip away with Ila to listen wide-eyed to her stories about the schools in the various metropolises of the world. Like roofs, verandas are not neutral spaces either. When Ila draws the plan of a house in the dust to play a game, the narrator is disturbed; 'It can't be a real house ... because it does not have a veranda. Of course we must have a veranda ... otherwise how will I know what's going on outside ... to me the necessity of verandas was no more accountable than the need for doors and walls.'

Ila's inability to understand this need ('what shall we do with a veranda') and the narrator's easy assumption of the inevitability of a roof as well as a veranda to make a house complete — both of which incidentally are enclosed spaces that provide access to the world outside — underline the essential difference between the cousins. Terraces and verandas, like courtyards, are essentially female spaces in our culture, and Ila's inability to comprehend their importance may at a realistic level be attributed to her upbringing in other countries, while at a metaphoric level this highlights her total self-absorption, living, as we are told, in 'an airlock in a canal, shut away from the tidewaters of the past and the future by steel floodgates'. Unlike the narrator, she does not need architectural spaces that connect her with the outside world, ensuring at the same time the privacy of interiority.

Houses have synecdochal relationships with countries in this novel, reconfirming the parallels between the family and the nation:

It was a very odd house. It had evolved slowly, growing like a honeycomb, with every generation ... adding layers and extensions, until it was like a huge, lop-sided step-pyramid, inhabited by so many branches of the family that even the most knowledgeable amongst them had become a little confused about their relationships.

Reminiscent of a poem by A.K. Ramanujan ('Small-scale Reflections on a Great House') where 'nothing that ever comes into the house goes out', where the haphazard and absent-minded inclusiveness gives the house and, by extension, the culture its identity, the Dhaka house in *The Shadow Lines* could also be read as a trope without invalidating its material reality. The construction of a nation is a two-way process, entailing on the one hand a broad homogenization, despite seeming differences, of what lies within the boundaries and a projection of alienness upon what is situated outside. The grandmother illustrates both these imperatives literally and metaphorically. Her attempt to reclaim family relationship with a branch that has long been estranged and its existence nearly forgotten is done with a grim, nearly ideological conviction: 'It doesn't mater whether we recognize each other or not. We're the same flesh, the same blood, the same bone ... ' Long ago, when the Jindabahar Lane house was partitioned, the children invented stories about the other half to highlight the strangeness and absurdity of the inversion of normalcy. The stories about the 'upside-down house' proliferated over the years and 'the strange thing was that as we grew older, even I almost came to believe in our stories'. In a novel where stories are accorded as much reality as lived experiences, this allegorizes the process whereby the identity of a nation is consolidated through imagined hostility with neighbours.

In *The Shadow Lines* there is a repeated insistence on the freedom for each individual to be able to create his own stories in order to prevent getting trapped into someone else's construction of reality. Tridib's early warning to the narrator —, that he should learn to imagine precisely — has to be seen in this context. Unless we invented our stories properly 'we should not be free of other people's inventions'. The novel makes visible the vulnerabilities of those who let themselves be appropriated unthinkingly by the various meta-narratives — be it the Eurocentric mastermyth of which IIa thinks she can be a part merely by joining the activists in rallies or the grandmother who clings to a notion of nationalism that rejects all those who live beyond the border. IIa and the grandmother are in many ways mirror images of each other across generations in their absolutism and rigidity about their own concepts of freedom and their situations in the novel are symmetrical. IIa is confident in her belief that history can only happen in Europe. What happens in India, Malaysia or Nigeria — 'famines, riots and disasters are local things after all ... nothing that is really remembered'. Her arrogance takes for granted the centrality of a western narrative that has been easily available to her and in which she has wanted to belong either as blue-eyed Magda or as a trendy Marxist. The grandmother on the other hand never had a ready-made script. Her genteel bourgeoise background was at odds with a secret desire to work for the terrorists; her struggle to lead an independent life after being widowed, her involuntary moves from Dhaka to Rangoon and then to Calcutta, her dispossession of the region she called home are discontinuous fragments of a story that can be made to adhere only by the moral glues of family and nation, duty and discipline. IIa calls her a fascist, but the narrator, borrowing the words of Tridib, describes her as 'only a modern middle-class woman — though not wholly, for she would not permit herself the self-deceptions that make up the fantasy world of that kind of person'. IIa's life on the other hand is a series of self-deceptions, from the stories woven around the school yearbook pictures to her last assertion that there is nothing wrong with her marriage, less justifiable because she is not a victim of history in as obvious ways as the grandmother is.

In the final section of the novel the narrator's desperate search in the archives to recover lost events has to be seen also as another example of insisting upon one's own story, a resistance to being swallowed up by narratives made up by others. The riots of 1964 which are indelibly engraved in his memory had by 1979 vanished without leaving a trace in histories and bookshelves. They had dropped out of memory into the 'crater of a volcano of silence'. The narrator needs to dismantle the public chronicle of the nation because it threatens to erase his private story.

At the heart of these intertwined stories that make up the texture of the novel there lies one untold story that cannot be plotted on any map:

It happened everywhere, whenever you wish it. It was an old story ... told when Europe was a better place, a place without borders and countries ... a man without a country, who fell in love with a woman across the seas ...

Tridib is promised this story as a birthday gift from Snipe but it is never narrated to him. As unstated allegory for the several love stories in *The Shadow Lines*, the resonance of silence around this Tristan and Iseult story is analogous to the withholding of details about the name and description of the narrator. Both stand in sharp contrast to the precision and concreteness of the other stories and the minuteness with which other allegories are followed through.

The house metaphor, for example, is worked out relentlessly by tying it up with the division of Bengal. The grandmother's expectation of the visibility of the border between India and East Pakistan grew indirectly out of her experience of the territorial divisions she had witnessed in childhood. When the ancestral home was partitioned, the brothers insisted on their rights with a lawyer-like precision so that the dividing line went through doorways and a lavatory 'bisecting an old commode. The brothers even partitioned their father's old name plate'. That the borders should be explicit, that the lines should be clearly marked on the land by 'trenches or something', was the least she could expect after so much violence and bloodshed during the partition of India in 1947. Yet, despite her insistence on the tidiness of separation we find her disregarding the imperatives of the division when she goes through a great deal of planning and danger to rescue a relative who belonged to the wrong side of the house ('It is a mirage; the whole thing is a mirage. How can anyone divide a memory?'). For her the family represented a moral order, the violation of which led to anarchy. The grandmother's fear of granting the narrator any resemblance with Tridib ('No, he looked completely different — not at all like you') arises out of her disapproval of Tridib's non-conformity, his refusal to accept family values. Her more virulent rejection of Ila can be explained by extending the syllogism from the family to the nation: Ila respects neither territorial not cultural frontiers.

The Shadow Lines obviously questions the idea of nationhood that is consolidated through the baptism of wars or coercive state apparatus. The grandmother valorizes apocalypses that make 'people forget that they are born this or that, Muslim or Hindu, Bengali or Punjabi: they become a family born of the same pool of blood'. Yet she does not fall outside the novel's inclusive ambit of sympathy; the author allows her historical position to confer a certain inevitability to her ideology. The representative of a class and a generation, in this novel she stands alone, as far away from her only son who is caught up in the upwardly mobile career graph of success, as from *his* only son who, in his fascination for maps and stories that would enable him to transcend space and time through the fluid sharing of other lives, is emulating the 'undesirable' example of Tridib. There is something haunting and illusory about the young man's desire for complete identification with Tridib, which, it is suggested at the end, is achieved through a woman who becomes a device for their bonding. Seen as a link with Tridib, May is seldom perceived as an autonomous person and her union with the narrator at the end despite the authorial avowals of a 'redemptive mystery' remains merely a rite of transformation of the young man. Even as May fills in some of the missing pieces in the Tridib story in a London coffee shop, their eyes meet in a mirror until at the climactic moment 'she turned away so that I could not see her eyes in the mirror'. As the narrator assumes Tridib's identity, May almost disappears.

Private and public narratives interpenetrate in the novel, history surging around ordinary lives to determine their colour and shape and both are perceived through the image of reflections in mirrors. The euphoria of nationalism that the Chinese War had generated in India in 1962 is seen as the mirror image of the exhilaration that the beginning of the Second World War had produced in England. Through a relayed recollection we know that it was the same in Germany 'though of course in a much more grotesque way. It was odd coming back here — like stepping through a looking glass'. Identical realities across territorial borders, which were originally meant to mark out differences, reiterate the theme of the novel as spelt out in its title.

During the 1964 Hindu–Muslim riots — subsequently forgotten by history — the panic that had gripped the schoolboys in Calcutta had 'the special quality of loneliness that grows out of the fear between oneself and one's image in the mirror'. The narrator's best friend, a boy called Mantu (Mansur) was suddenly transformed into an enemy. Subsequently the two governments traded a series of 'symmetrical' accusations as if in a mutual narrative of complicity regarding the riots, while the people on both sides reacted with an 'identical' sense of horror and outrage as there were 'innumerable cases of Muslims in East Pakistan giving shelter to Hindus, often at the cost of their own lives, and equally in India of Hindus sheltering Muslims'. The 'looking glass border' attempts to create a mirage of otherness but only sees itself reflected.

The apparently simple narrative of *The Shadow Lines* is in fact a complex jigsaw puzzle of varied time and place segments including some magic pieces that mirror others. The last fragment in this puzzle does not fall into place until the end when Robi unravels the mystery of Tridib's death. His nightmarish tale concludes with a meditation on the chimeric quest for freedom on which both state violence and terrorist activity are directed. As a civil servant he has to exhort his subordinates to kill 'for our unity and freedom' and when on returning home he receives a note from the terrorists that he has to be killed for *their* freedom it is like 'reading my own speech transcribed on a mirror'.

The reiterative use of the two images — mirrors and maps — interact in the novel to stretch the narrative beyond mimetic realism to incorporate an element of mystery, a bafflement at the frontiers of knowing. The child who had once believed that distance separates, 'that it is a corporeal substance ... that across the border there exists another reality', has by the end of the novel had some of these certainties shattered. Bartholomew's Atlas is for him no longer a safe guide to a neatly compartmentalized world; the solid lines dividing countries turn into glass, through which it is clearly visible that Chiang Mai in Thailand is spatially closer to Calcutta than New Delhi, Chengdu in China is nearer than Srinagar. The material world represented by maps has not changed, nor is it suggested that immigration queues, customs barriers and visa regulations can be wished away, but the familiarizing perspective in *The Shadow Lines* initiates an interrogation of the organizing principles of division.

8

Haroun and the Sea of Stories: Fantasy or Fable?

A children's story about a sinister carnivorous bird would seem an unlikely choice for inclusion in a high-profile literary anthology, but the presence of Satyajit Ray's 'Big Bill' (the original title in Bangla is 'Brihat Chanchu') in Salman Rushdie's *The Vintage Book of Indian Writing*, a commemorative volume for the golden jubilee of India's freedom, is explicable only when seen in the perspective of Rushdie's long-time interest in Satyajit Ray.[1] No anthology is ever objective; each attempt to bring together representative texts from a country/period/language/genre is destined to become an exercise to validate the editor's own position through the construction of a personalized canon — witness for example the wilful conflating of Indian Writing in English with Indian Literature in *The Vintage Book*. The inclusion of 'Big Bill' in this volume reflects Rushdie's personal predilection for Ray's work, particularly the bizarre and fantastic aspects of his imagination — both in film and fiction — testified through many indirect references in Rushdie's novels, a whole essay in *Imaginary Homelands* and multiple echoes in *Haroun and the Sea of Stories*. This essay attempts a reading of *Haroun*, using the Ray element in it as the starting point. The parallels between these two storytellers, one intensely and controversially political and the other the last of the

humanist artists of our century who eschewed political engagement, may not however stretch too far, but occasional links illuminate the text.

Most people outside the Bangla-language region know Ray as
the maker of serious films like *The Apu Trilogy* (1955, 1956, 1959),
Jalsaghar (The Music Room, 1958) *Debi* (1960), *Ghare Baire* (The
Home and the World, 1980) and many more. But within his own
language community he has a huge and enthusiastic following as a
children's writer and a film-maker in the comic mode. His children's films include *Goopy Gayen Bagha Bayen* (1968), *Sonar Kella*
(1974), *Joi Baba Felunath* (1978) and *Hirak Rajar Deshe* (1980).
The dozens of books he wrote for children in at least three different
genres — detective stories, science fiction and comic tales —
continue to remain at the top of the best-selling list even today,
seven years after the author's death. Rushdie, by declaring *Sonar
Kella* (The Golden Fortress) as one of his favourite movies, is said
to have made Ray feel like 'the proud parent whose least appreciated child has been lavished with unlooked-for praise' (*Imaginary
Homelands*, p. 11). The praise must have been 'unlooked for'
coming as it did from a 'non-Bengali' (a blanket term often used
in Bangla to lump the rest of the world as 'not us') because the
local critics had always been enthusiastic about the film and, along
with *Goopy Gayen*, *Sonar Kella* has remained the favourite of two
generations of children and adults. The film critic Chidananda
Dasgupta explains the enchantment thus: 'Ray's children's films
have a secret core of joy, a Mozartian Magic Flute quality in which
the children are little Papagenos, unimpressed by evil, which is a
cloud that only makes the sun shine brighter.'[2] This is also the
iridescent quality that permeates Salman Rushdie's only children's
book *Haroun and the Sea of Stories*, and the affinity is worth a closer
look.

In an interview Ray was once asked a question that bordered
on an allegation: Why did he in his children's film *Goopy Gayen*

Bagha Bayen allow the effervescent mode of fantasy to get congealed into a fable by the end?[3] The same charge has been obliquely
brought against Rushdie by many reviewers of *Haroun and the Sea
of Stories* (1990), a text where I suspect Ray's influence extends far
beyond the occasional borrowing of proper names. *Haroun* too
has been seen as a moral and aesthetic parable dressed in the garb
of a children's story. *Haroun* appeared one year after Ayatollah
Khomeni's fatwa (14 February 1989) and the allegorical relationship between a story-teller who has lost his power to create and a
writer who has been sentenced either to silence or to death was
too strong for the critics to pay attention to the fantasy or fun
element in the tale. Ray did not see any dichotomy in the two
modes: 'I am not sure a clear demarcation can be made between
the two. Fantasy ... meaning the use of the supernatural and the
magical can be part of the fable and the two can merge naturally'
(*Ray*, p. 33).

An attempt has been made here to examine the process or the
possibility of this merger, not only of the two narrative modes,
fantasy and fable, but of several other concerns — moral, aesthetic,
political, ecological and intertextual — that are allowed to converge in this slender tale meant for children. Before doing so, let
me explore briefly the Ray–Rushdie connection.

The plentymaw fish in *Haroun* who speak in doggerel verse are
called Goopy and Bagha — pointing our attention to one of the
many pre-texts from which *Haroun* draws. The purpose stories
serve in Rushdie's novel is analogous to the function of songs in
the film *Goopy Gayen Bagha Bayen* (*GGBB*), both countering the
principles of silence, suspicion and strife with a celebration of art,
articulation and consequently, of life.

Like the battle between the lands of Gup and Chup in *Haroun*,
the action in *GGBB* climaxes in the battle between the two nations
Jhundi and Shundi (the people in Shundi have lost their speech)
and eventually Goopy and Bagha are able to stop the war through

their songs, bringing back peace, harmony and voice. Rushdie too in *Haroun*, as in all his other novels, valorizes a plurality of voices, privileging polyphony over an enforced unity of silence.[4] Paradoxically, heterogeneity is seen as more cohesive than the monolithic idea of a nation. In the uneven battle between the Guppees and Chupwalas, the Guppees have the advantage of possessing multiple voices. 'All those arguments and debates, all that openness, had created powerful bonds of friendship between them' (185), while 'the vows of silence and the habits the secrecy had made (the Chupwalas) suspicious and distrustful of each other' (185). Most characters in *Haroun* outside the dark land of Chup have their distinctly different ways of speaking — the fish speak in rhyming couplets, Mali speaks in quatrains, Mr Butt's sentences are punctuated with 'but, but, but' and 'no problem', General Kitab's speech is peppered by a series of innocuous oaths ('stop and blast me', 'spots and fogs', 'drat it all', 'dash it', 'rot it all' etc.), Prince Bolo uses the cliched rhetoric of romance while Princess Baatcheat communicates through execrable love songs — all contributing their bit to a lively din of heteroglossia.

In Ray's film this heteroglossia is to be found in its musical score, natural in text where not stories but songs carry the theme forward. Although Goopy and Bagha mention in a song that they are simple folk who know no other language but Bangla, it is clear very soon that the verbal content of the songs is incidental to the communication of their meaning. What is more important is that Goopy and Bagha know the language of music that transcends speech. In any case the people of Shundi do not speak at all, so Goopy and Bagha would not know what language they understand. Hence they plead 'True, you may not understand what we speak, but we hope that what we sing, even if it is not intelligible, will travel through your ears and reach your hearts' (*Ray*, p. 37).

The unorthodox music of *GGBB* freely incorporates elements from western symphony, Hindustani classical as well as Carnatic

music and Bangla folk tunes, using a whole range of string instruments — cello, ektara, dotara, violin (sometimes played so as to
sound like 'sarinda', a folk instrument of East Bengal) — and twelve
types of percussion instruments — mridangam, ghatam, tabla,
khanjira, murshrinka, etc. Visually, too, this plurality is sustained
in the well-known ghost-dance sequence in the film where varieties
of ghosts — fat and thin, black and white — (actually they are
bhoots; the Bangla word 'bhoot' with its slightly comic connotation
is inadequately translated as 'ghost') are choreographed together
in an eerie yet hilarious ballet. Ray explains his design thus:

I thought of those who lived and died in Bengal and became its resident
ghosts — people of diverse roots and races ... kings and chieftains as well
as tillers of the soil right from the Buddhist period, as also the Englishmen
of John Company. (*Ray*, p. 39)

This multiplicity is replicated in the sea of stories that Rushdie's
text *Haroun* conjures up, where several streams coexist, the title
itself invoking at least two traditions of narrative cycles — the
Arabian Nights from West Asia from which the name Haroun
originates, and *Katha-sarit-sagar*, a compendium of stories in
Sanskrit attributed to Somadeva who lived in Kashmir in the
eleventh century. The name of the caliph of Baghdad, Haroun-al-
Rashid, gets split into the names of the father and son, invoking
the cycle of tales that for Rushdie has long been a synecdoche for
an inexhaustible storehouse of stories. Even six years after *Haroun*,
Scheherezade returns on the last page of *The Moor's Last Sigh*. But
in *Haroun* the houseboat called 'Arabian Nights Plus One' also
shades into the *2001 Space Odyssey*, deliberately bringing in the
ambience of science fiction (the resolution of the plot is after all
predicated upon making a planet turn), and the story of Prince
Bolo and Princess Baatcheat weaves in a'parodied romance rhetoric — yet another diverse strand — of knight errants and damsels
in distress. Both Ray's film and Rushdie's story are thus celebrations of plurality.

In *Imaginary Homelands* Rushdie has paid tribute to Ray in an essay (107–14), but a passage in *The Moor's Last Sigh* reveals more about Rushdie's natural preference for the fantasy films of Ray over his realist ones, even though the film-maker now gets a fictitious name:

> The great Bengali film director Sukumar Sen ... was the best of those realists and in a series of haunting humane films brought to Indian cinema — Indian cinema, that raddled old tart! — a fusion of heart and mind that went a long way towards justifying his aesthetic. Yet these realist movies were never popular ... and Vasco (openly) and Aurora (secretly) preferred the series of films for children in which Sen let his fantasy rip, in which fish talked, carpets flew and young boys dreamed of previous incarnations in fortresses of gold (173).

The final reference in the last sentence is obviously to another children's film by Ray, *Sonar Kella*, and the flying carpet is evidently a trope to signify all fairy tales. But the talking fish would puzzle even the most knowledgeable viewers of Ray's films unless they have also read *Haroun* because Ray's films never show any fish, talking or otherwise. The rhyme-spouting fish in Rushdie's novel (Goopy and Bagha) have derived their names from the singing heroes of *GGBB*, and by a sleight of syntax Rushdie gives back to Ray what he has received from him, in the process conflating *Haroun* with *GGBB*.

Like Vasco and Aurora in *The Moor's Last Sigh*, Rushdie clearly prefers fantasy to mimesis. This novel articulates in various ways the basic aesthetic position on which his entire oeuvre is based — suspicion of the literal and the realist, and a faith in the epic–fabulist mode which, according to him, can do justice to 'the narrative of our magic race and the dream-like wonder of our waking world' (*Moor*, 173). *Midnight's Children* and *Shame* chronicled the recent history of our subcontinent in the extravagant language of fantasy with intermittent and indirect references to Bombay films, another realm of the non-real. In *The Moor's Last Sigh*, continuing with the film allusions Rushdie makes the painter Vasco urge Aurora, a greater artist, not to attempt naturalism which might be the mode of nation-building, because it stifled creativity:

Will you spend your life painting boot-polish boys and air-hostesses and two acres of land? Is it to be all coolies and tractor drivers and Nargis-y hydro-electric projects from now on? ... Forget those damnfool realists! The real is always hidden ... inside a miraculously burning bush! Life is fantastic! Paint that ... [5]

If *GGBB* and *Haroun* are both parables of art, one focusing on songs and the other on stories as the specific metaphor for creativity, *The Moor's Last Sigh* has a comparable agenda, but it uses painting as its dominant trope. The sea of stories here turns into a carnival of canvases, extravagantly proclaiming the inadequacy of mimesis for representing life which is never completely rational. *Haroun* makes it apparent that if the real world is full of magic, the magic world could also be real — and 'fearsome too' — as the dedication to the novel alerts us. Fantasy in children's fiction hardly needs justification since it has always been the staple of fairy tales. As a professed practitioner of the non-realist mode of narration, Rushdie is hardly 'an unlikely children's writer' as Judith Plotz supposes,[6] because while only the sophisticated adult readers take to his kind of 'magic realist' fiction, children, never surprised by miracles or incredulous of metamorphoses, enjoy this mode of narration most naturally. They find it easy to accept metaphors as literal truth (as in 'the sea of stories') and when actual events are turned into metaphors, a transformation frequently achieved in *Haroun*, they readily take that in their stride. This playful inter-changeability may be an end in itself, a jugglery that entertains by its virtuosity (as did Rashid's stories, and Haroun did think of his father as a juggler), it does not necessarily preclude fable as Satyajit Ray had insisted in his interview and as Judith Plotz agrees by the end of her paper: 'every stylistic feature contributes to the poetics of fun, but it is simultaneously politics ... In this endlessly and rapidly talkative book the fun talk is also freedom talk.' In a comparable manner the comic extravagance and musical energy in *GGBB* are not diminished by the anti-war fable of friendship and amity that emerges at the end. Since the march of the warring king's army in *GGBB* is presented in a staccato and comic manner, reminiscent of Chaplin's *The Great Dictator*, several critics sought a parallel with Nazi Germany — a link that is historically improbable in a story written in 1915 by Upendra Kishore Roy Choudhury (Satayjit's grandfather) and perhaps ideologically not very relevant in a film made in 1968. However, the Chaplinesque style may have been used by Ray as a comic device for caricaturing tyranny, as indeed has been done with parodic self-consciousness by lesser film-makers since then.[7] In reading *Haroun* or watching *GGBB* children are entertained by the fun element while adults may find the attempt to decode the allegory more challenging, but the possible simultaneity of the two enterprises gives both texts their durable richness.

In a disarming interview on ABC Radio (Sydney) on 10 December 1995, Rushdie insisted that he was primarily a comic writer, revelling in the absurdities and humorous possibilities of life. His disavowal of a serious agenda behind the rhetoric of comedy may be disingenuous, but perhaps understandable at a moment when the temptation to superimpose Rushdie's biography — which has probably passed into post-modern history now — seems to override all other considerations in discussing his books. Even though a young poet in one of his earlier novels had proclaimed that the writer's job is 'to name the unnameable, to point at frauds, to take sides, start arguments, shape the world and stop it from going to sleep' (*The Satanic Verses*, 97), we find Rashid, the archetypal artist in *Haroun*, happy enough merely to entertain his audience and bring some cheer into their gloomy lives. But he has to do this in his own way and not be dictated by the government's policy of propagating 'up-beat praising sagas', even though he does not make an issue of it — as did Baal 'the proud and arrogant' young poet in *The Satanic Verses* who stiffened at the proposal of writing political verse and retorted: 'It isn't right for the artist to become the servant of the state.'

Rashid is not interested in these larger issues. Once he is connected to the wellspring, the unending stream of stories pour out of him most naturally, hinting at the magic and fluidity of their under-water origin, a source which the reader gradually discovers with *Haroun*. The fairytale incandescence with which the literal ocean is turned into a metaphoric sea of streams of stories is achieved simply by translating from Sanskrit the title of one of the 'earliest and largest collection of short stories extant in the world' (Banerji, 215), consisting of 18 books of 124 sections or *tarangas* (waves). In this ocean, streams/stories of different colours constantly weave in and out of each other as liquid tapestry:

... as all the stories that had ever been told and many that were still in the process of being invented could be found here, the ocean of the streams of story was in fact the biggest library of the universe. And because the stories were held here in liquid form, they retained the ability to change, to become new versions of themselves, to join up with other stories and become yet other stories, so that unlike a library of books, the ocean of the streams of story was much more than a storehouse of yarns. It was not dead, but alive. (72)

What may in abstract terms be called the self-renewing attributes of narrative become concrete when we find the plentymaw fish constantly swallowing the water into their many mouths and spewing out new ones, incorporating bits and pieces of the old stories.

There could not have a more vivid metaphor for the playfulness and regenerative power of fancy. At a time when Rushdie in real life was pushed into a realm where the fictive was seen as literal, and all exercises of the imagination were suspect, he needed the relatively safe space of a children's book to make his statement about freedom and laughter, sport and normalcy, magic and reality. But the genre of children's literature is not a subterfuge, it is in fact the most appropriate genre for articulating these ideas because children most readily accept this co-relation while some adults like Mr Sengupta in the Sad City do not see the point of stories 'that are not even true'. If Rushdie knew Bangla, he would have counted the likes of Mr Sengupta among the 'offspring of Ramgarud' — a category that seems to be custom-made for him. Ramgarud is a creature invented by Sukumar Ray (incidentally, he was Satyajit Ray's father) in a comic verse that has passed into Bengali folk mythology. The children of Ramgarud are forbidden to smile. Disapproving of all mirth, they live in perpetual terror of the lurking whiffs of laughter which might infect their lungs.[8]

Haroun is a story about stories, narrated through the adventures of a boy who undertakes a journey to restore to his father his lost gift of story-telling. The allegorical core of the narrative points to the essential tension between those who celebrate the imagination and those who feel threatened by its energy. Khattam Shud the arch-villain, who looks like Mr Sengupta but is more diabolical in his scheme of destroying all stories, is asked by the intrepid Haroun:

"But why do you hate stories so much? ... Stories are fun ... "
"The World however is not for Fun", Khattam Shud replied. "The World is for Controlling."
"Which World?" Haroun made himself ask.
"Your World, my world, all worlds", came the reply.
"They are all there to be Ruled. And inside every single story, inside every Stream in the Ocean, there lies a world, a story world that I cannot Rule at all. And that is the reason why." (161)

But this antithesis between art and power (be it political or re-ligious) is not in itself entertaining; it has to be enlivened by comic action and by the vivacity and the verbal dexterity of the narrative — punning, word games and bi-lingual semantic juggling. Rushdie delights his young readers in the Indian subcontinent (most of whom do not need the glossary at the end) by the sheer inventiveness of the names of characters — Butt and Iff (Butt is a perfectly credible Kashmiri name and Iff can be the abbreviated form of names like Iftikar), Chattergy the King (a common Bengali name which in English rendering gets split into 'Chatter' and the respectful suffix 'ji'), Princess Battcheat and Prince Bolo. All of them, along with Blabbermouth, are associated with the prolixity of speech, eponymously celebrated in the name of the city of their residence — Gup. But the land of Chup on the dark side of Kahani is full of negative names suggesting silence: the field of Batt-mat-karo, the cult-master Bezaban, the arch-villain Khattam Shud. Because stories are made of words there is a textuality in the entire fabric of Guppee society and even in their institution of the Army, where soldiers are called 'pages'; they are organized in 'chapters' and 'volumes' and wear laminations on their body. When the infantry meets under the leadership of General Kitab there is a loud rustling of 'pages' until order is established through proper 'pagination' and 'collation'.

Even the topography of the novel is textual, or rather alphabetical, the country being Alifbay (comprising the first two letters of the Arabic alphabet), thus subtly linked with the Xanadu invoked in the dedication where Alph the sacred river ran. Like the river in Xanadu the places in the land of Alifbay have alphabets for names. The valley of K once had another name which might have been Kache-mer (a place that hides a sea) or Kosh-Mar (nightmare) — transparent variations on names of the troubled valley of Kashmir, Rushdies's own land of origin — a place conjured up in the text by a host of not-so-subtle hints — Dull lake (the lake in Kashmir is spelt 'Dal'), and the spectacular view of the valley as one came out of the 'Tunnel of I which was also known as J' (Jawahar Tunnel at Banihal) with 'its fields of gold (which really grew saffron) and its silver mountains (which were really covered in glistening, pure, white snow and its Dull Lake (which didn't look dull at all)' (39).[9]

Use of verbal and textual tropes for foregrounding the primacy of language in story-telling is to be found in abundance in Rushdie's work. One sustained and extravagant example can be cited from *Midnight's Children*, describing the unborn Saleem's growth as a foetus in his mother's womb:

... what had been (in the beginning) no bigger than a full stop had expanded into a comma, a word, a sentence, a paragraph, a chapter; now it was bursting into more complex developments, becoming, one might say — a book — perhaps an encyclopaedia — even a whole language. (115)

It is not only verbal play that delights the young reader, but also the eccentricities of the characters and the amazing exploits of the young hero, the old-fashioned tale of whose barehanded bravery to save his father merges into the apparatus of a science-fiction quest in which the secret of moving a planet has to be discovered.

In the mythology of this tale, the earth's second moon Kahani has a dark and a bright side. The dark half is silent while the other is bubbling with voices. As in the ghost-dance sequence in *GGBB*, black and white get reversed in the land of Chup: 'They all had the strange reversed eyes, with white pupils instead of black ones ... and blackness where the whites should have been' (148). Haroun who inadvertently gets involved in the battle between the two is struck by the number of opposites that confront each other in this war: 'Gup is warm and Chup is freezing cold ... Guppees love the ocean, Chupwalas try to poison it. Guppees love stories and speech: Chupwalas, it seems, hate these things just as strongly' (125). Evidently, the struggle is also between life and death; between clean air and pure water on the one hand and a polluted landscape and an acid sea on the other. Just as in the Sad City, inhabited by men like Sengupta, 'black smoke poured out of the chimneys of the sadness factories and hung over the city like bad news', the Chupwalas were infecting the live ocean with the virus of anti-stories manufactured in the poison factory located in a black ship — trying eventually to plug the well-spring — the original source of all stories which lay directly under the ocean bed. *Haroun* may be a parable of art and its enemies but it is ingeniously dovetailed with contemporary ecological concerns linking the restoration of creativity with saving the ocean from pollutants.

In *GGBB* the evil magician who brewed the drugs to keep the two brother kings apart belonged to the world of fantasy, while Khattam's poison factory in *Haroun* with its devices of 'converting mechanical energy into electrical energy by means of electromagnetic induction' belongs to the realm of science fiction. Haroun is aided by a bird with a brain-box with memory-cell and command modules; he has a 'bite-a-lite' torch to illuminate his path, but ultimately what saves him, rescues Princess Baatcheat and purifies the ocean is not technology or science-fiction strategies, but a bottle of 'wish-water' of pure fairy-tale variety. The power of this magic potion could finally combat all the 'immense supercomputers and gigantic gyroscope that had controlled' the movements of the planet. The wish-water from the magic world finally vanquished the science fiction world because it 'possessed a force beyond [their] power to imagine, let alone control' (172).

Once the moon begins to move, the solidity of shadows melts (like 'ice-cream left out in the sun', or like butter or cheese softening in the heat), exposing ultimately the insubstantial nature of evil. In the epigraph to *The Satanic Verses* Rushdie had quoted a passage from Daniel Defoe's *The History of the Devil* which referred to Satan's 'empire in the liquid waste or air' without any solid anchoring place on the earth. Haroun's act of will counters the shadowy machinations of Khattam Shud who is as dull[10] as he is unreal, and as the moon starts to move, light and dark, silence and speech become dialogic again.

Thanks to Haroun's mediation, Princess Baatcheat is rescued, the ocean is saved, normalcy restored and 'peace breaks out'. But the fable of the battle is framed by two other stories — of the family and of the state. The novel begins in the Sad City where Haroun lived with his once-happy family, then moved onto the valley of K where he travelled with his father at the invitation of Mr Buttoo whose unpopular government was trying to use stories to win the next election. Gup's victory over Chup has to be re-enacted in these two frame stories also, before the book can have an ending satisfactory to children who do not like loose ends hanging. An interweaving of the stories is attempted through pairs of identical characters (Sengupta and Khattam Shud, the bus driver Butt and the Hoopoe bird with a mechanical brain) and a conjunction of incidents (the wishing water that enables Haroun to achieve the double miracle of making Kahani resume its lunar movement and prevent the well-spring of stories from being plugged, also in addition restoring his father's subscription to story-water). The story that had got blocked at the political rally in the valley of K gets finally told at the end. Rashid's story that inspires the people to rise against the oppressive ruler is also called 'Haroun and the Sea of Stories', demonstrating in a tangible way the thesis that stories can be a cohesive force in constructing a community. So far the synthesis of the fabular and the political is seamlessly done. But beyond the fabular and political there is a personal story about a family, and Rushdie's real problem must have been the intractability of the family story in this general atmosphere of joy and jubilation.

Rushdie's dedication of this book to his son Zafar in acrostic verse is very much a part of the text, providing clues to the adult reader for reading the story. The dedicatee is about as old as Haroun, Haroun's father's name is a close anagram of that of

Zafar's father. Both the fathers — fictive and real — have suffered the loss of voice. So far as the biography remains in the public domain, the situation can be allegorized, and the different levels — romance (king/prince/war/rescue of princess), science fiction (AP2C2E, the instrumentation centre) and politics (Snooty Buttoo, his armed bodyguards and his election campaign) — be made to merge, creating a delightful fantasy where a young boy, Pinnocchio-fashion, is able to rescue his father. But the story of a child's sadness over his parents' broken marriage is too personal to be allegorized and resolved at a stylized level. The Manichaean binaries of dark and light, speech and voice, do not work at this level and therefore the happiness of Haroun and Rashid's return to their own city acquires a greater patina of fantasy than their sojourn in the fabulous land of Kahani. The rains bring joy, Haroun's mother comes back, the house is full of her songs and all is well again. Thus, the flourishing of art is seen as coterminous with the well being of life. Misfortunes had started when Haroun's mother's songs and father's stories had simultaneously dried up; felicity returns when both are restored, even though the account of only one restoration is narrated to us. The other cannot be told because it lies outside the realm of childrens' fiction.

The second line of the acrostic — 'All our dream-worlds may come true' — makes space for this elision, deliberately locating the book at the level of a wish-fulfilment fantasy. If in the magic world Haroun can be the saviour of his father through deeds of adventure, in the real world the son can rescue him through the act of reading: 'As I wander far from view/Read and bring me home to you' urge the last lines of the dedicatory verse. But the text is not only the site for the mutual reclamation of father and son, it is also a political arena for contesting coercive erasure and an ethical space for asserting the final insubstantiality of evil that only children's stories can make with impunity.

Notes

1. *The Vintage Book of Indian Writing 1947–1997*, ed. Salman Rushdie and Elizabeth West (London: Random House, 1997). In the Introduction Rushdie mentions including only one translated piece: an Urdu short story by Saadat Hasan Manto. He does not refer to the fact that Satyajit Ray's story 'Big Bill' was originally written in Bangla and published in *Aaro Baaro* (Calcutta: Ananda Publishers, 1980).

2. *The Cinema of Satyajit Ray* by Chidananda Das Gupta, first published 1980 (New Delhi: National Book Trust, 1994), p. 84.

3. 'Many have complained that *GGBB* starts as fantasy but ends as a fable. In the beginning it is propelled by the logic of absurd or fantastic story-telling, but midway becomes sermonizing and moralizing, splitting the story into two unlike parts', *Ray in the Looking Glass: Two Interviews*, p. 32.

4. Rushdie's novel *The Moor's Last Sigh* may be read as a lament on the transformation of a multivalent metropolis called Bombay to a city intolerant of those outside the majority culture.

5. *The Moor's Last Sigh*, p. 174. The references are to a number of films of the fifties: Raj Kapoor's *Boot Polish* and Bimal Roy's *Do Bigha Zamin* for example. 'Nargis-y dam' refers to Nargis's complaint about Ray portraying poverty and not projecting modern India. When the interviewer asked her what was modern Indian, she replied 'Dams ... ' Rushdie quotes this in *Imaginary Homelands*, p. 109. The veiled allusion may also be to Mulk Raj Anand's early novel *Coolie* and social realist fiction of his kind.

6. In a yet unpublished conference paper Judith Plotz argues that Rushdie 'consistently (even self-servingly) has positioned himself as an *important* public writer with large political and social ambitions, one who writes of a sphere from which childhood concerns are largely banished ... '. Only after the fatwa, she observes, Rushdie is marginalized like children and children's writers. 'And Rushdie, liberation writer that he is, since the Ayatolla's fatwa has become a pent-up constricted, subject, suddenly infantalized, or at any rate, bechilded.' Plotz's premise is that children's literature has historically been produced by marginalized and often disempowered writers, frequently women. This may be true of children's literature in English, but incidentally the situation is quite different in Bangla, the language in which Satyajit Ray made his films and built up an enormous reputation as a children's writer. All the major (male) writers including Rabindranath Tagore have written for children. This however does not affect the validity of Plotz's argument regarding Rushdie.

7. For example, in *Sholay*, a popular Hindi film of the seventies, a tyrannical prison warden is made to walk like Chaplin's *Great Dictator*.

8. This poem appears in the volume *Aabol Taabol* by Sukumar Roy, reprinted numerous times in the last six decades.

9. It is curious that Aaron Ali in his erudite paper on the significance of names in *Haroun* dwells on the semantic implications of 'Kache-mer' and 'Kosh-Mar' without mentioning that they play upon the name of a well-known place name on the real map of the Indian subcontinent.

10. The dullness of evil is underlined by the repeated linking of Khattam Shud with clerks: ' ... a skinny, scrawny, snivelling drivelling, mingy, tingy, measely, weasely, clerkish sort of a fellow' (190). It may be recalled that his counterpart in the Sad City — Mr Sengupta 'was a clerk in the offices of the city corporation and he was ... sticky-thin and whiny-voiced and mingy ... ' (19).

References

Ali, R. Aaron. '"All Names Mean Something": Salman Rushdie's *Haroun* and the Legacy of Islam'. *Contemporary Literature*, 36 : 1 (Spring) 1995, pp. 103–29.

Banerji, Suresh Chandra. *A Companion to Sanskrit Literature* (Delhi: Motilal Banarsidas, 1971), p. 215.

Plotz, Judith. '*Haroun* and the Politics of Children's Literature.' Unpublished paper presented at a seminar in Washington in 1993.

Ray in the Looking Glass: Two Interviews. Introduced by Jyotirmoy Datta. Translated from Bangla by Kankabati Datta and Vidyarthi Chatterjee (Calcutta: Badwip, 1993).

Rushdie, Salman. *Haroun and the Sea of Stories* (London: Granta, in Association with Penguin, 1990).

—— *Imaginary Homelands* (London: Granta and Penguin, 1991).

—— *Midnight's Children* First published 1980 (New York: Avon Books, 1982).

—— *The Moor's Last Sigh* (London: Jonathan Cape, 1995).

—— *The Satanic Verses* (London: Viking Penguin, 1988).

9

The Anxiety of Indianness

In 1938 a young Indian writer living in France wrote an experimental novel in English which carried a succinct Foreword of three paragraphs. This Foreword seems to have been an early diagnosis of the theoretical issues involved in this bicultural act. If we can scrape off the patina of obviousness that has gathered over this statement in the six decades that have intervened, it may be possible to examine the relevance of its implications today, at a time when English novels written by Indians have suddenly gained more visibility than ever before in the brief span of our relationship with the English language.

I call it brief because in the long history of Indian literature(s) writers in English are the latest arrival, some might even say interlopers, and certainly people who have taken their shoes off and made themselves at home. But the metaphor may not be quite appropriate because writers in English need not take their shoes off to be comfortable: they keep them on because they are, at least potentially, among those whom *Time* magazine calls 'the new makers of World Fiction',[1] whose raw material may be in India, but whose target readership spans countries and continents, keeping them ever-ready to undertake journeys — either real or figurative. Taking off your shoes will not do when you have to travel these days.

The Foreword mentioned above was written by Raja Rao when his novel *Kanthapura* was published in London six decades ago. Not only did he experiment with language in this novel, striving to make English take on the cadence of Kannada as spoken by women in the Kara district of Karnataka, evoking occasionally the rhythm of Sanskrit, but also with narrative mode, challenging the generic expectations of the novel as prevalent in western Europe in the 1930s. He used the form of a 'sthalapurana', the legendary history of a village caught up in the Gandhian movement as told by an old woman — thus trying to integrate myth with history, realism with fabulation, linearity with a cyclic notion of time long before post-modernism made such enterprises trendy. In the heyday of modernism, with its implicit ideology of the alienation of the artist and the deliberate separation of art from mass culture and community life, this novel predictably did not get much attention in England; and then as now the Indian reception of the book, or lack of it, invariably reflected the attitude out there. It is only decades later that the novel was resurrected and 'canonized' in India. The Foreword alerts us to Raja Rao's self-reflexivity in undertaking this project:

The telling has not been easy. One has to convey in a language that is not one's own the spirit that is one's own. One has to convey the various shades and omissions of a certain thought movement that looks mal-treated in an alien language. I use the word 'alien', yet English is not really an alien language to us. It is the language of our intellectual make-up, like Sanskrit or Persian was before — but not of our emotional make-up.[2]

Having said this, Raja Rao goes on in the text to pollinate this intellectually acquired language of formal discourse with memory, myth, oral tales and gossip to capture the texture of daily existence, the quarrels and alliances, the smell and sound of a village on the slopes of the Sahyadri mountains, where life is determined not by the clock or the Gregorian calendar but by seasonal rhythm. The national movement for freedom gets narrativized not through accepted historical modes of chronology and records, but by adopting an indigenous model of validation through stories, a practice kept alive by women. I single out Raja Rao for mention not only because he is the first to articulate the anxieties of the Indian novelist in English in his prefatory remarks, but also because in the text he works out a strategy for negotiating the contesting claims of language and culture.

II

If I were to write a novel in Marathi, I would not be called an Indian writer in Marathi, but simply a Marathi novelist, the epithet Marathi referring only to the language, not conveying the larger burden of culture, tradition and civilization. No one would write a doctoral dissertation on the Indianness of my Marathi novel. But when it comes to English fiction originating in our country, not only does the issue of Indianness become a favourite essentializing obsession in academic writings and the book-review circuit, the writers themselves do not seem unaffected by it, the complicating factor being that English is not just any language — it was the language of our colonial rulers and continues even now to be the language of power and privilege. It is not a language that permeates all social levels or is used in subaltern contexts. Our discourse on Indian novels in English tends to get congealed into fairly rigid and opposed positions. When an earlier version of this paper was orally presented in Delhi, the audience, both general and academic, was much more interested in my position in the cultural war between the global and the regional, between English for the world market and Hindi/Bengali/Marathi, etc. for an indigenous and therefore presumably more 'authentic' readership than in looking at them as disparate literary products of a complex plural culture.

The unspoken premise in this war is that writing in English and writing in the other Indian languages (hereafter referred to as 'bhasha')[3] are antithetical enterprises marked by a commitment to, or betrayal of, certain undefinable cultural values. To me the issues are far more complex, entangled with questions of class, mobility and readership. It is not easy to demarcate cultural categories in India, but it may be said that there tends to be an element of urban/mofussil divide in the matter of linguistic choice. That is, of course if language is at all a matter of choice. I cannot imagine any Indian — whether Punjabi, Bengali or Oriya — one day making a deliberate decision to write in English because it would guarantee him a wide audience and ensure access to the literary reproduction system of a world market, hence yield royalties in foreign exchange. Those who write in English do so because — no matter what language they speak at home — they have literary competence only in English. Contrary to popular belief, not all of them achieve fame abroad, and it is possible that some are read by numerically fewer people than read a bhasha novel. It may be more useful for us to understand the circumstances that lead to the loss of the mother tongue than to charge these writers for capitalizing on their loss.

If any one has a choice, it is the occasional bhasha writer — never the one who is writing in English. Most people would agree that writers like Agyeya, Buddhadeb Bose, B.S. Mardhekar, Krishna Baldev Vaid, U.R. Anantha Murthy, Gauri Deshapande, Nabaneeta Deb Sen, Mrinal Pande and many others could just as well have chosen to write in English. It they did, whether they would have evolved differently from what they are now would always remain a hypothetical question. But the more pertinent question to ask is would their children (figuratively speaking) opt to write in their mother tongues, and if not, what are the pressures that compel them to choose differently? What has changed in the last decade or two? My attempt here is to analyse the cultural implications of the Indian English novel, not to praise or bury it.

Indian writing in English as a recognizable literary phenomenon becomes visible only in the 1930s (the earlier attempts failed to make an impact for reasons I have tried to explore in the first essay of this volume), and the first generation of writers, as a ballast to the supposed alienness/elitism of the language, tended to deploy certain thematic or formal devices to tether their texts to indigenous contexts. This compensatory act was not necessarily undertaken self-consciously, nor was the effect always obtrusive. Mulk Raj Anand's anger at the class and caste inequities in a hierarchic Hindu society, Bhabani Bhattacharya's exposure of religious charlatansim, Kamala Markandaya's concern with the suffering of the unspecified 'Indian' woman — are as much illustrative cases of this anxiety manifested in themes as are the efforts of Raja Rao, G.V. Desani and Sudhin N. Ghose in narrative mode. The latter try in different ways to dismantle the constraints of the written novel to achieve the meandering freedom of the oral narrative. It is necessary to understand the process historically, even though not all these writers deserve equal attention, because out of this uneasy collusion between language and sensibility a few remarkable fictional texts have emerged.

Among this older generation of writers R.K. Narayan has had a fairly steady and wide readership at the popular level — augmented in the late eighties and nineties by a delightful television serial based on his stories — and at the literary level bolstered by the glossy editions of his novels that appeared in London and New York. For decades Malgudi has been perceived as a quintessential Indian town, ordinary and uneventful, where shopkeepers ply their easy-going trades, idlers sit around the Market Street gutter, benign crooks go about their business of cheating gullible people, husbands absent-mindedly torture their wives — all in a gentle and unchanging rhythm. If complications arise, they are bound to be resolved by the end and normalcy restored. What is always emphasized is its 'Indianness', by which is meant a good-humoured inertia and a casual tolerance which almost any reader in the country is expected to recognize as familiar. Like other imaginary towns in literature we do not know the latitude and longitude of Malgudi, nor do we know its different languages, its ethnic or communal tensions. Whether a character is called Swamy or Sen, Krishnan or Pal, Daisy or Kamala, s/he belongs to a harmonious Malgudian milieu, except occasionally when the man who has come from Junagarh is allowed to be more aggressive than the one from Mangala. Malgudi is Hindu upper-caste pan-India, resistant to change, eternal and immutable — very different, say, from Maryganj in Phanishwar Renu's *Maila Anchal* (Hindi: 1954) or Purnea in Satinath Bhaduri's *Jagori* (Bangla: 1946), both in north Bihar, variegated in terms of caste and subcaste, language and dialect, and in the throes of constant turmoil. Or Shivpalganj in Srilal Shukla's *Raag Darbari* (Hindi: 1968), which is so convoluted in its power equations that it subverts the comfortable pastoral connotations of the rural–urban dyad, commonly seen in simplicity/sophistication and spontaneity/artifice polarities. The visitor from the city is completely baffled by the complications of Shivpalganj. As examples of spatial specificity and the resultant complexity of social and cultural configurations it is possible to cite examples from Mahasweta Devi's fiction also. Her powerful stories about tribal life are always located — in Tohar, Palani or Lohardaga — their conflicts subtly implicated in the local ethnic, class, gender and language dissonances. While reading her, we know exactly where Lohri is situated — at the intersection of three districts of Chotanagpur — Ranchi, Palamau and Sarguja — and this is not a gratuitous piece of information.

I am neither trying to privilege ethnographic documentation in fiction over other aspects, nor insisting that mimetic representation should always be the desired narrative mode, but merely suggesting that in the English texts of India there may be a greater pull towards a homogenization of reality, an essentializing of

India, a certain flattening out of the complicated and conflicting contours, the ambiguous and shifting relations that exist between individuals and groups in a plural community. This attenuation may be artistically valid when the narrative aspires to the condition of allegory but for the Indian writer in English there may be other unarticulated compulsions — the uncertainty about his target audience, for example.

An O.V. Vijayan or Bhalchandra Nemade knows his exact constituency and is secure in the knowledge of the shades of response his associative word-play or ironic understatement will evoke in the Malayalam or Marathi readers who are equipped with the keys for decoding these oblique messages. But R.K. Narayan's audience is spread far and wide, within India and outside, hence the need for an even-toned minimalist representation that will not depend too much on the intricacies and contradictions in the culture and the inflections of voice which only an insider can decipher.

Of course it can be argued that Narayan has the humour and talent to convert all these constraints to his advantage. V.Y. Kantak once compared his style to the one-stringed instrument made of clay which used to be sold on the streets to children. The man who sold it could play any tune on it, but having brought one you could never replicate his feat. In his bare, unadorned, understated manner Narayan achieves quite a range of effects not possible for others to emulate, but an one-stringed instrument, even in the hands of the master, cannot become a sitar or a veena.

III

For a long time it had seemed that English writing in India was destined to remain an one-stringed instrument, because the normal ground conditions of literary production — where a culture and its variations, a language and its dialects, centuries of oral traditions and written literature, all interact to create a new text —

do not exist in the case of English in India. Take for example the case of Malayalam, which is not only the spoken and written language of the geographic space called Kerala with oral variations among different groups — the Nairs, Nambudris, the Christians, the Mapillas, etc. — but also the language of its films, both commercial and serious, its songs, folk tales, riddles, nonsense verse, nursery rhymes, proceedings in the Vidhan Sabha, slogans in processions, rhetoric of political speech, conversation on the football field, street-corner humour as well as of Kathakali and a long literary culture. A fictional text that is produced in this language today draws upon, and echoes, the reverberations of this layered plurality that surrounds and nurtures it. English in India on the other hand functions on relatively fewer registers and it would not have been surprising if this remained a permanent liability, allowing the novelists to operate only within a limited parameter.

The themes handled by the older generation of novelists in English had for a long time remained predictably pan-Indian: the national movement, partition of the country, the clash between tradition and modernity, faith and rationality or similar time-worn cliches of east–west confrontation, disintegration of the joint family, exploitation of women, etc. In this project they were in a way defining 'Indian' concerns as against local or regional issues. All students of literature are aware how the novel as a genre has traditionally been implicated in the construction and consolidation of the idea of the nation. The history of the English novel in Britain from *Robinson Crusoe, Tom Jones, Mansfield Park, Jane Eyre* to *The Forsyte Saga* and *Brideshead Revisited* is a chronicle of the discourse of the nation, the totalization of British culture through a dissemination of ideas that construct the field of meanings and symbols associated with national life, at the same time differentiating it from what is not British. The Indian novel in English has also in its brief history been visibly concerned with defining such a national identity. It may not be a coincidence that the novel in English emerged in India in the 1930s, the decade prior to independence, when there was an urgency to foreground the idea of a composite nation. In colonial India — in the nineteenth and early twentieth century — English was not a major language of literary production. It was the language of administration and higher education while the novel flourished in Hindi, Urdu, Bangla, Marathi and other bhashas. Only towards the end of the imperial chapter do we find isolated fictional attempts in English, slowly (but not steadily, because there have been occasional fallow periods) gaining momentum to become a dominant presence by the last decade of the century.

The three pioneering writers who began their careers almost simultaneously in the 1930s (and who continue to be productive and prolific after a half a century)* may have been worlds apart in their ideology, background and narrative modes, but they shared an unspoken faith in a distillable Indian reality which could then be rendered through particularized situations. In *The Serpent and the Rope* Raja Rao constructed an advaitic brahmanic India; Anand's novels on the other hand exposed the claims of this high culture by taking up the cause of the paradigmatic Indian under-class. R.K. Narayan's Malgudi, I have already argued, had a met-onymic relationship with India as a whole.

Any project of constructing a national identity is predicated upon two simultaneous imperatives: an erasure of differences within the border and accentuating the difference with what lies outside. As a language English in India automatically achieves the first, and the second is facilitated when a homogenous Indian tradition is pitted against an equally unified imaginary west. It is worth noting that in this dialectic of alterity the non-western countries (in Asia and Africa) never had a part to play until a few years ago when Amitav Ghosh and Vikram Seth brought

* R.K. Narayan passed away in 2001, one year after the first edition of this book was published.

them in, though marginally — through their fictional as well as non-fictional work — by writing about Egypt, Cambodia, Burma and Tibet. The schematic and metaphysical polarization of the east and the west, common in the middle decades of our country, is seen not only in the novels of Raja Rao but also in those of Balachandra Rajan, Kamala Markandaya and Bhabani Bhattacharya.

The contrasts do not operate so sharply in the subsequent decades. Despite a few prominent writers emerging in the 1960s (or a little before and after) — like Nayantara Sahgal, Anita Desai, Arun Joshi — who are all very different from each other, the 1970s were a relativity barren decade (except for the work of one novelist, Shashi Deshpande), and for a while it almost seemed that this sub-genre of the Indian novel had run out of steam and come to the natural end of its brief life. But then came the explosion of the 1980s.

The 'tradition' of Indian writing in English is discontinuous; there is no genealogy that can be traced satisfactorily, however much scholars might attempt to create one. A young man or woman in Bombay or Delhi who has a half-written manuscript in English inside the desk — and there are scores of such closet writers today — aspires to be part of a global league, and not contribute to some outmoded category called the Indo-Anglian novel. These young people may have drawn literary inspiration entirely from the English or American books studied in the classrooms and European or Latin American novels borrowed from libraries, or from Rushdie or Kundera — without ever taking the trouble to find out how Indian writers of an older generation responded to the creative urge in English. It goes without saying of course that they hardly have any acquaintance with bhasha literatures. Yet, paradoxically, if they achieve any fame abroad it will be on the basis of their relationship with India and their ability to find new modes of representing the complex reality of their own culture. Alternatively, these aspiring writers may have spent a few years abroad, or have settled down in some other country, thus qualifying to be part of the 'displaced', 'diasporic' migrancy, to belong to which is becoming almost mandatory for the Indian writer in English. In that case they write about their mixed heritage with the lost country looming large in the mosaic. There is no getting away from the burden of India if you want to write in English.

IV

It is generally agreed that the sudden profusion, liveliness and visibility of the new Indian fiction in English in the 1980s can be traced back to the success of one seminal novel: *Midnight's Children* (London, 1981). Rushdie celebrated the plenitude of India in what came to be labelled as the post-modernist mode, but even those not schooled in the latest in literary theory recognized that several assumptions about language, nation, history and narrative mode were being challenged here. In retrospect we see that *Midnight's Children* had a very important role to play in the reversal of the 'centre–periphery' paradigm in English literary culture, in dissolving the great tradition of F.R. Leavis into a plurality of traditions, coming from many races, many regions, many cultures. But even if one did not take a global view, the novel offered the Indian reader a playful and imaginative representation of his own recent history and remembered public events that could open out to different kinds of readings. It could be read as a narrative where the abundant multiplicity of India is threatened by the bleak forces of binary opposition. On the other hand it could be read as a novel where the obsessive fear of fragmentation assumes a concrete shape in the cracks and fissures that appear in human bodies and on the map, prefiguring a total disintegration.

Images of mutilation and holes pervade the novel, beginning with the perforated sheet through which the doctor was permitted to examine the female patient, anticipating the many partial views of reality the novel plays with, and going on to show the country splitting up amoeba-like first into two and then more pieces. But there is also the inclusive image of the MCC — the parliament of children where all the languages, religions and ethnic identities co-exist as in All-India Radio. Saleem is nostalgic about the India of his childhood where 'he was beset by an infinity of alternative realities' and critical of the Pakistan of his adolescence where this choice was denied through the forced binariness of truth: right and wrong, black and white, friend and enemy.

There may be an element of comic and parodic exaggeration in the rendition of an easy co-existence of diversity in the land of his birth, encapsulated for example in *Amar-Akbar-Anthony* fashion, in the varieties of mothers Saleem has: biological, adoptive and nutrient — Vanita, Amina and Mary Pareira, and the many fathers he acquires through life — British, Hindu, Muslim, Sikh — but this playfulness does not go against the central project of the novel.

Although in an entirely different way from the earlier novels, *Midnight's Children* is also constructing the idea of a nation — an India that is inclusive and tolerant — and the novel is beset with an anxiety about the fragility of this concept of India. (Rushdie's later novel *The Moor's Last Sigh*, 1995, reads like an elegy for this lost ideal.) The narrative ends with the declaration of Emergency in 1975 when the inclusive principle fails, the binary antinomy comes to prevail. As Shiva comes to power and Saleem is marginalized, the comic ebullience darkens. But at this point of the end there is also another kind of beginning. Because Saleem Sinai is on the verge of disappearing, he feels compelled to record the past. The act of writing becomes a cathartic effort at recapturing his control over the world through language: 'This is why I have resolved to confide in paper.' Hence the importance of memory — often fallible — and the centrality of the pickle factory where fruits in bottles, like truth in books, are being preserved against the 'corruption of the clock', even though the colour and the flavour change in the process.

Rushdie's example — his inventiveness, his irreverence, his audacity, and above all his success — became liberating for a large group of Indian writers living either at home or abroad. At first many of them seemed to be Rushdie clones, but over the years unusual writers with distinct voices have emerged, many who do not have more than only a vague family likeness to him. Collectively the younger writers have been able to enter the discursive space in literature which in the western world was earlier reserved for the privileged race. But there is a discursive space in India too — not confined merely to the Sunday supplements of English dailies and chat shows on television channels; what place do these writers occupy there when they are seen in conjunction with young writers in the Indian languages? Or are they never seen in relation to each other? As I have mentioned earlier, there is a tendency to see these writers (in English and bhasha) in opposed camps, partly out of an awareness in the disparity of their fame and fortune — not necessarily in proportion to the disparity of talent. But surprisingly, *Desh*, the magazine of the Bangla literary establishment, of late has been very enthusiastic about claiming some of these novelists who have earned famed abroad, perhaps partly out of a regional chauvinism, because many of the new writers have names that mark their Bengali origin.[4] It is indeed a curious phenomenon, because a cultural group based on language solidarity seems suddenly eager to appropriate those who have achieved fame by severing connection with that language.

V

In 1989 Timothy Brennan proposed a new category of novelists: the 'Third World Cosmopolitans', who are globally visible, whom the reviewers in *New York* and *London Review of Books* hail as interpreters and authentic voices of the 'Third World'.[5] According to Brennan, this group includes Mario Vargas Lhosa, Derek

Walcott, Salman Rushdie, Isabel Allende, Gabriel Garcia Marquez and Bharati Mukherjee, but not Chinua Achebe or Wole Soyinka. If he wrote his book a few years later he might have added the names of Ben Okri, Robert Antoni, Michael Ondaatje and a few others. The Third World cosmopolitans emerge from a non-western culture, but their mastery over the current idiom of the metropolitan meta-language of narrative ensures their favourable reception in the global centres of publication and criticism. It should also be noted that not all outstanding writers from other cultures (writing in English or translated into English) receive this attention. The new receptivity in London or New York may have made it easier for some writers from outside the western world to get a hearing, but they may do so only within a field of reception already defined by metropolitan parameters and agendas. The criteria of evaluation are naturally selective, determined by the demands of the recipient culture.

One implicit expectation from Third World cosmopolitan writers (also known as postcolonials) is that they will highlight the experience of colonialism as theme or metaphor — as for example Rushdie did in the Methwold part of *Midnight's Children*. Even at the time of his departure from Bombay, Methwold made sure that the furniture, the painting and the other objects of the house would remain unchanged, a plot device used by the author to underline the continuing impact of a way of life (and thought) imposed by the rulers which gradually becomes part of one's own. Postcolonialism, a burgeoning branch in academic studies, initiated incidentally by countries that have not been at the receiving end of the imperial process in the recent past, privileges colonialism as the framework for the major cultural experience of the century, and it is these academies now that set the terms for critical debates and creative enterprise in the world. Yet we know that in very few of the major works of fiction in the Indian languages is colonialism any longer an important concern. Far more pervasive has been, for example, the theme of partition and writers in at least four languages of the country (Hindi, Urdu, Bangla and Punjabi) have gone back again and again to this rupture to understand our present. Many other forms of internal dissension, dislocation and oppression engage the attention of the bhasha writer today, relegating the trauma of colonial experience to the background. From my limited reading I would venture to say that even in the past, barring an unusual novel like *Gora* (Bangla: 1909) which is a long reflection on identity, nationality and the impact of colonialism, most of our fictional literature has been conditioned by other, either older or newer, more local, diverse and complex pressures and intricate social hierarchies than can be explained entirely by British rule in India.[6] This may be one reason why many of our bhasha classics — past and present — even when translated into English, do not get noticed either by the academic establishment or the publication/distribution system outside the country.

Many of the books that have been taken up for discussion in this system recently happen to be those that have successfully manipulated western forms — fabulist narratives and a post-modernist mode with local legends and popular fables as a means of mythicizing contemporary reality. Another issue to which value is attached in the West these days is cultural hybridity, which is said to offer certain advantages 'in negotiating the collisions of language, race and art in the world of disparate people comprising a single, if not unified world'.[7] Experience of rootlessness and displacement are thus privileged in the cosmopolitan discourse. Ondaatje (born in Sri Lanka, educated in England, lives in Canada) describes his fictional characters darkly as 'international bastards, born in one place, choosing to live elsewhere. Fighting to get back to or get away from our homelands all our lives',[8] while Bharati Mukherjee (born in India, lived in Canada, lives in USA) joyously celebrates her mixed heritage:

I have joined imaginative forces with an anonymous driven underclass of semi-assimilated Indians with sentimental attachment to a distant homeland, but no real desire for permanent return ... Instead of seeing my Indianness as a fragile identity to be preserved against obliteration (or worse, a 'visible' disfigurement to be hidden) I see it now as a set of fluid identities to be celebrated ... Indianness is now a metaphor, a particular way of comprehending the world.[9]

Indianness remains important for her, but only as a metaphor India less as a place than a topos, a set of imaginative references.

But the problem is that for those who live at home, who are not global migrants, the reality of India has to be daily confronted at a non-metaphoric level. Henry Louis Gates Jr. has an amusing anecdote about himself and another black colleague coming out of an academic seminar where 'blackness' had been discussed as a literary trope, and not being able to get a taxi in downtown New York. 'But it is only a trope', they shouted to the taxi-drivers; but that did not make any of them stop.[10] India may be a 'discursive space' for the writer of Indian origin living elsewhere, but those living and writing here, particularly the bhasha novelist, would seldom make figurative use of something as amorphous as the idea of India, because s/he has a multitude of specific and local experiences to turn into tropes and play with.

VI

If the anxiety of Indianness in Raja Rao, Anand and Narayan came out of their own desire to be rooted, the anxiety of the new generation who can thrive on easy international accessibility may be attributed to the pressures of the global marketplace which demand that Upamanyu Chatterjee's *English, August* — a zany existential comedy — be subtitled 'An Indian Tale', and Shashi Tharoor's playful intertextual exercise *The Great Indian Novel* be perceived as a national allegory. As Aijaz Ahmad has pointed out, even in India there seems to be developing a new urban culture

... for whom only the literary document produced in English is a national document. All else is regional, hence minor and forgettable, so that English emerges in this imagination not as one of the Indian languages, which it undoubtedly is, but as the language of literary sophistication and bourgeois civility.[11]

Newspapers and journals often discuss the phenomenon of the new Indian novel in English merely as the 'New Indian Novel' as if other languages do not matter, and in April 1993 a two-part television programme was shown on the national television channel on 'Publishing in India' which assumed English as the only language in which publishing is done in India. This amnesia about Indian languages whose texts in any case have a longer history and a large numerical presence is not an accident. It is part of a cultural change overtaking us that covers an area larger than the domain of literary production. Elitism, for example, is no longer an allegation to be avoided or a burden to be alleviated by a conscious identification with the 'people', or concern with political or ideological issues. Part of the appeal of Upamanyu Chatterjee or Amit Chaudhuri for the younger generation may be located in their unapologetic acceptance of their exclusive upbringing, which some of these readers share and the others aspire to.[12]

The demands of economy, both national and global, create a thrust towards a homogenization of culture, and in India the language that can most effectively achieve this is English, which is also the language of upward social mobility. The sudden communication revolution that has brought international television channels inside urban homes is helping to spread this amnesia where the culture constructed by the media, the advertisement and entertainment industry — a slicker and more attractive package than what real life in India can offer — is successfully obliterating the local and the regional sub-cultures unless they are brought back as 'planned authenticity' or the exportable ethnic. English is being spoken, at least partially, in more upper middle-class homes than ever before, kinship terms are simplified to suit a supposedly western model, and clothes, behaviour patterns, footwear and leisure activities are geared towards an international norm. It is logical that reading habits should also follow this trend. Whether it is desirable or not, seen from this point of view, the growing visibility of English as the preferred language of literature in India seems to be an irreversible process. We shall probably encounter more and more writers who will write in English, propelled by the logic of social dynamics within the country, lured by the forces of global marketplaces and driven by the mirage of international fame.

But genuine writers as a species are individualistic in any language refusing to fall into predictable models. This is one reason why the imperatives set up by multinational publishing corporations in complicity with the metropolitan institutions that determine fictional standards may not always succeed in controlling and directing our literary production. Vikram Seth's *A Suitable Boy* may have been an international best-seller, but it became so entirely on terms set by the author, not the publisher. Reading the manuscript before publication, I remember wondering if anybody except a reader like me who shares the same regional background would get so completely involved in the nuances of the story of these interlocked upper middle-class families in UP, Bihar and Bengal. We know that the author is familiar with Jane Austen and Dickens and George Eliot, and advertisement hype even linked the book with *War and Peace*, but for me, his novel might just as well have been written in Bangla where a tradition exists of long three-decker realistic stories about families.[13] This tradition, most probably shared by other Indian languages also, is marked not by any anxiety but by a confident prolixity. Perhaps this point is further proved by the easy assimilation into the Hindi literary world of the recent translation of *A Suitable Boy* (*Koi Achcha sa Ladka*, tr. Gopal Gandhi, 1998). A critic as biculturally perceptive as Harish Trivedi has commented on how the novel naturally flows into Hindi while *Midnight's Children* (*Aadhi Raat ki Santanen*, tr. Priyadarshan, 1998), according to him, fails to pass this acid test of translation.[14] Trivedi goes to the extent of admitting that at times the Hindi translation 'merrily surges ahead and outstrips the original'. This is possible, he thinks, because *A Suitable Boy* is 'most deeply embedded in the theme and the context which it depicts and the most intimately complicit in a local language'. Perhaps 'languages' in the plural will be a better description, because a distinctive quality of *A Suitable Boy* is its polyphonic mosaic. Despite the initial impression of the novel being entirely documentary without verbal resonance, the variety of linguistic registers it plays with turns out to be wide-ranging. Ghazals of Mir, Ghalib, Vali Dakkani and Mast are as easily embedded in the text as are the nonsense verse of Sukumar Ray, *chaupais* from *Ramacharit-manas*, parodied lines of *Rabindra sangeet*, long passages of *Mar-siya* at Muharram, as well as Landor's epitaph for Rose Aylmer. The rustic Urdu spoken at Debaria is made to sound different from the courtly grace of Saeeda Bai's conversation, and Haresh Khanna's studied English is evidently worlds apart from the casual doggerel-spouting wit of the Chatterjee family in Calcutta. In an unobtrusive way Seth manages to capture the linguistic diversity of Indian life even though he is writing in English.

As a different kind of example I will mention Amitav Ghosh's *The Shadow Lines* (1988), to me the one novel written in the 1980s that will survive all the rest that appeared in that boom decade.[15] The novel betrays no anxiety because it attempts to prove nothing and interrogates rather than defines the concept of a totalizing India. The narrator speculates tentatively on the varieties of human freedom and the bonds across space and time to explore personal relationships. India is neither a metaphor nor a philosophical idea. Calcutta and Dhaka are concrete places, so are New Delhi and London, but the boundaries between countries that arbitrarily separate people to congeal their identities in rigid shells are seen as illusory tricks that politics plays with human history and natural geography. The book glows with the light of a cartographic imagination and Bartholomew's Atlas plays not a small part in it.[16] Ghosh's geographic inclusiveness is free of anxiety about roots and cultural ties. As in the works of the best Indian language writers today, words like 'marginality' and 'hybridity' seem irrelevant here and segmenting the world into first and third regions a rather absurd activity. The Indian novelists to be taken seriously are the ones not conditioned by the pressures of the global market. If they succeed, they do so as individuals, unfettered by the burden of otherness.

Notes

1. 'The Empire Writes Back', Pico Iyer, *Time*, 8 February 1993, pp. 46–56.

2. Foreword to *Kanthapura* (1938; Bombay: Oxford University Press, 1947).

3. I am borrowing this usage from G.N. Devy (*After Amnesia: Tradition and Change in Indian Literary Criticism*, Bombay: Orient Longman, 1993). It is more convenient to use bhasha as a generic term instead of mentioning every time the names of the languages, e.g. Hindi, Bangla, Marathi, etc. Using the term 'Indian languages' may be misleading because English too is an Indian language. Bhasha refers to the modern languages of India other than English.

4. For example, Amitav Ghosh, Bharati Mukherjee, Upamanyu Chatterjee, Amit Chaudhuri; also, the old stalwart Nirad C. Chaudhuri. One enthusiastic commentator in *Desh* even claimed Vikram Seth as a Bengali because he was born in Calcutta. When *The God of Small Things* appeared in 1997, there was an attempt to call Arundhati Roy a Bengali as well, because of her last name.

5. Timothy Brennan, *Salman Rushdie and the Third World* (New York: St Martin's Press, 1989), p. 34.

6. See Aijaz Ahmad's cogent arguments on this issue in *In Theory: Classes, Nations, Literatures* (London, Verso, 1992; rpt Delhi: Oxford University Press). Specially relevant is chapter 3.

7. Quoted in *Salman Rushdie and the Third World*, p. 35.

8. Quoted in the *Time* magazine article cited above.

9. Bharati Mukherjee, Preface to *Darkness and Other Stories* (Harmondsworth: Penguin Books, 1995).

10. Henry Louis Gates Jr., *Loose Canons* (New York: Oxford University Press, 1992), p. 47.

11. *In Theory*, p. 75.

12. Salman Rushdie's statement claiming that the post-1947 Indian writing in prose 'both fiction and non-fiction ... is proving to be a stronger and more important body of work than most of what has been produced in the eighteen "recognised" languages of India, the so-called "vernacular languages at the same time" (*The Vintage Book of Indian Writing 1947–1997*) was not published when this paper was written, but already, in the early nineties, ignorance of bhasha literature was beginning to be regarded as a mark of sophistication.

13. While reading *A Suitable Boy* I caught myself remembering several massive novels in Bangla that I enjoyed in my youth, particularly Buddhadeb Bose's *Tithidor* (the title means marriage) which is also woven around the theme of a girl choosing a suitable husband from the limited options available to her. More generally, Seth's novel can be related to the voluminous trilogies by Ashapurna Debi and Bimal Mitra (beginning with *Pratham Pratishruti* and *Saheb Bibi Golam* respectively). Parallel examples from other Indian languages may not be difficult to find. Incidentally, the recent Bangla translation of *A Suitable Boy* (*Satpatro*, 1999, tr. Enakshi Chatterjee) has been very well-received by the Bengali reading public.

14. Harish Trivedi, 'Translation as Recovery: *A Suitable Boy* as *Koi Achcha-sa Ladka*', and 'Rushdie into Hindi: *Midnight's Children* on Native Ground', *The Book Review*, September 1998 (pp. 30–31) and December 1998 (pp. 35–7).

15. Whether *The Calcutta Chromosome* (1997) will assume the same status in relation to the novels of the nineties is too early to say, but Ghosh's extraordinary new novel dismantles in a radical way many assumptions one has so far associated with English writing in India.

16. I am tempted to trace this back to Bibhutibhusan Banerjee, whose Bangla novels *Pather Panchali* (1929) and *Aparajito* (1931) are replete with a similar fascination with geography. Young Opu's imagination is fired as much by the tales of Mahabharata as by a poem about the German soldier who thinks of his village Bingen on the Rhine, the stories of the sunken ship off the coast of Porto Plata and typhoons in the China Sea. At the end of *Aparajito*, the adult Opu sets sail for South America, an unusual destination for an Indian in 1931 when the book was published. Another novel by Banerjee, *Chander Pahar*, is set almost entirely in Uganda.

10

Divided by a Common Language

Translations have always been a vital part of Indian literary culture even when the word 'translation' or any of its Indian language equivalents — *anuvad, tarjuma, bhashantar* or *vivartanam* — were not evoked to describe the activity. The *Ramayana* and *Mahabharata* have been retold in almost every Indian language, and stories not only from Sanskrit but Arabic and Persian also have freely travelled from region to region through adaptations and modifications. Folk tales circulate in India, as they do all over the world, paying scant heed to language boundaries. In the early era of the novel in India, many novels from England were indigenized in our languages sometimes with necessary modifications to give them a local habitation and a name. Translations, adaptations, abridgements and recreations were overlapping activities and it was not considered important to mark their separate jurisdictions. I grew up reading abridged children's classics in Bangla — ranging from *The Iliad, Sindbad the Sailor, Les Miserables, The Three Musketeers* and *Twenty Thousand Leagues Under the Sea*, many of which, I am ashamed to admit, I never went on to read either in the original or in fuller versions in later life and did not feel particularly deprived.

What has changed in the situation is that now we are focusing on translation as a field of study rather than as part of the natural ambience we live in. It is certainly a more self-conscious act today, and is being discussed more than ever before; in 1998, for example, there have been no less than half a dozen seminars, workshops and conferences on translation in India, some of which I have attended, others I have heard about. In the last quarter of the twentieth century an academic discipline has evolved — first in the European and North American universities, and now gradually making its way to our shores — which concerns itself with the semantic, cultural and political issues involved in the act of linguistic transfer and its history through the centuries. As in other disciplines, in the humanities and social sciences in India, only much more so in Translation Studies, scholars cannot get very far by being derivative of its western model. The complex linguistic dynamics within the country and the ambivalent position of English in present-day Indian culture (simultaneously a local as well as global medium) create, along with porous language boundaries[1] and many other factors peculiar to India, a unique configuration that cannot be analysed by existing translation theories originating in Europe. But first, we need to gather a great deal of empirical data on the situation in India before theoretical tools of our own can emerge.

Even without statistical surveys, certain diachronic changes in translation practice in India seem fairly apparent. The translation of novels from one Indian language to another (and here I am going to look at novels only), which was a major conduit of cultural transmission within the country for nearly a century, seems to have declined in recent decades to make way for a new activity which is fast growing in visibility — the translation of Indian language fiction into English. In the early part of the twentieth century Marathi readers knew Bankimchandra Chattopadhyay through direct translations from Bangla and Harinarain Apte, a major early novelist in Marathi, would have been known in the neighbouring regions in Kannada or Telugu versions. Lalithambika Antherjanam (1909–88) acknowledges the early influence not only of Rabindranath Tagore's novel *The Home and Outside* on her writing, but of a much less known Bangla writer Sitadevi Chattopadhyay on her Malayalam writing.[2] I have met several North Indian readers who casually assumed that Saratchandra Chatterjee was originally a Hindi writer — such was the widespread availability of his novels in translation, and his grass-roots popularity in regions outside Bengal. In my classroom in Jawaharlal Nehru University (Delhi) where a cross-section of selected students come from all over the country, even in the late 1980s I used to come across an occasional student from Kerala who knew Premchand's *Godan* or Tarashankar Bandopadhyay's *Arogya Niketan* through Malayalam translation, but such readers are far fewer today than they were a generation ago.

To me this decline is a matter of regret for several reasons. Transferring a text — say from Hindi to Bangla or from Marathi to Kannada — is a far more natural and satisfactory activity both for the translator and the reader than when the same novels are rendered into English, where negotiating semantic and cultural hurdles to achieve equivalence of meaning tends to be a relatively uphill task. I say this in full awareness of Edward Sapir's statement that 'No two languages are ever sufficiently similar to be considered as representing the same social reality' (p. 69). It is true that even neighbouring languages do not inhabit identical universes but intersecting penumbras of meaning between two languages in the subcontinent are likely to generate a richer resonance of recognition and discovery than the against-the-grain 'elevation' into the master language of the world with certain inevitable attenuation of specificity. The target audiences are also very different in each case. The potential readers for an English translation of, say, a novel by Shivarama Karanth or Manik Bandhopadhyay would be an indeterminate and undifferentiated mass, situated either in the same region or in another part of India. Among them some may have rural hinterlands in their background not entirely unlike what these writers draw their material from, or they may be cosmopolitan urban Indians in the metropolis with no exposure, either direct or literary, to subaltern Indian life. Or the reader may be in another country altogether, with no previous knowledge of the ethos being represented. As a result, the anxiety of communication gets reflected in an explicatory or dilutionary tendency. But the translation, say from Gujarati into Hindi or from Oriya into Bangla used to be undertaken for a very specific and well-defined audience, and consequently the nervous uncertainty about decoding culture would be less evident. Moreover, when a local language text gets translated into a global and economically stronger language like English, there is an implicit and inevitable hierarchy involved in the process. As Susie Tharu and K. Lalita have pointed out: 'translation takes place where two, invariably unequal worlds collide, and ... there are always relationships of power involved when one world is represented for another in translation' (p. xxii). Since most Indian languages (hopefully) occupied roughly parallel spaces in our culture, specially in relation to the master space occupied by English, the politics of power might have played a lesser part in these mutual translations. It would however be simplistic to assume that all the Indian languages, either in their own self-perceptions or in perceptions of each other, had equal partnership in a common literary endeavour. The discrepancy in the numbers of translations from and into a particular language is one of the indices of this inequality. For example, many Bangla novels were translated into Kannada, Malayalam, Telugu and Marathi, but the reverse did not happen. But by and large that does not substantially alter my statement that translation among Indian languages used to be a major literary activity in the past.

I speak in the past tense not because such translations have ceased altogether, but because they are no longer perceived as important in the respective languages while every English publisher in Mumbai, Chennai or Delhi is hastening to add titles in translation to their existing catalogues to keep up with the times. Only in the realm of drama the state of mutual translation continues to be relatively healthy and vigorous. Perhaps the general dearth of good plays in India makes the theatre world conscious of the need to share whatever is available. Mohan Rakesh, Vijay Tendulkar, Badal Sircar, Girish Karnad, Mahesh Elkunchvar, G.P. Deshpande, Satish Alekar and now Mahesh Dattani travel from language to language with ease, to be performed successfully in different parts of the country, although not all these translated scripts achieve the permanence of printed books.

But in the genre of the novel mutual translation is now by and large a neglected literary activity, while a growing number of people — many of them connected with English teaching at the college and university level — are trying their hand at translating Indian-language texts into English. Some amount of translation activity does continue in languages like Hindi and Malayalam, traditionally more hospitable to texts from other parts of India than some other languages, and over the decades these languages have been enriched by this ready receptivity. In contrast Bangla is a poorer language to the extent that, although eager to translate from European literature, it has been stubbornly resistant to contemporary writing from the rest of the country. The alleged literary superiority of Bangla is a matter of history now, but the arrogance perpetrated by that myth continues to the present day. The few available Bangla translations from Tamil, Urdu or Marathi are all officially undertaken projects, sponsored by the Sahitya Akademi or the National Book Trust, hence reflect neither popular interest nor literary predilections.

In 1996 when a three-cornered project called Kaveri–Ganga was launched as one of the many activities of the *Katha* imprint to produce direct translations among three languages — Bangla, Tamil and Kannada — the real difficulty turned out to be identifying bilingual translators.[3] Evidently proficiency in Indian languages is no longer the marker of sophistication and culture as it had once been in India. The few capable translators located after an intense search turned out to be all elderly and retired people. Among the metropolitan youth today, even among those interested in literature, literary knowledge of even one Indian language — not to speak of two — is considered redundant if one has proficiency in English. Global monolingualism is the aspiration of the younger generation today.

In July 1997 the Kaveri–Ganga project succeeded in producing three slim but excellent volumes in three languages — Tamil, Kannada and Bangla. But amid the din of publicity of books with bigger marketing budgets, not much has been heard of this modest venture, even in the respective languages. Books are noticed and read not necessarily because of their intrinsic quality; their success often depends on strategies of publicity and distribution. Hence books translated from one Indian language to another may never compete with translations into English which have, to begin with, an all-India urban market, and potentially a bigger one in other English-speaking countries.

However, once we accept the inevitability of this change as the consequence of globalization, instead of merely regretting the decline in mutual translations we should also be looking into the positive potential of this publication boom of English translations from Indian-language fiction. Hypothetically, Bhalchandra Nemade's Marathi novel *Kosla* (in English translation *The Cocoon*) or O.V. Vijayan's Malayalam novel *Khasakinte Ithihasam* (in translation *The Legend of Khasak*), both much acclaimed in the 1960s in their respective languages, now become available not only to Indian readers who do not read Marathi or Malayalam, but also to readers in Australia, Canada, Britain or USA should they want to read these books. How widely this is actually happening is a question worth considering.

It is not that English translations of Indian fiction are an entirely new phenomenon, but, barring a few exceptions, until the sixties of the twentieth century it had been like a sporadic cottage industry — the author himself or his friends attempting amateurish translations of isolated texts and bringing out limited editions privately — which were hardly ever commercially distributed. In the sixties came a few organized ventures, by Jaico Paperbacks, Hind Pocket Books, and Asia Publishing House. There was also an excellent series sponsored by UNESCO which made well-known novels like *Pather Panchali, Umrao Jan Ada, Chemmeen, Garambicha Bapu* and *Putul Nacher Itikatha* available in English. But that was a trickle compared to the spate we are witnessing now. Except for the UNESCO project, which in any case did not originate here, Indian publishers in the sixties did not display much professionalism in their enterprise. Very rarely would there be an attempt to introduce the author or the text or to provide a suitable frame to help the uninitiated reader. Sangam Paperbacks, an imprint of Orient Longman, in the seventies were the only exception, and might have, without too much fanfare, paved the way to the more systematic activity we have been witnessing in the next two decades. There is now a careful selection — or at least a semblance of it — of the texts to be translated, an attempt to provide a suitable context for each text through an Introduction, Translator's Preface and Notes, and a consciousness about the need for quality control over the texture of the language. The latter however is an activity fraught with controversy. It seems the policy of certain translators to achieve smoothness and readerly ease at any cost while others take a deliberate position that the language of translation must contain syntactical as well as lexical reminders that the source text comes from another culture. One recalls that the editors of the influential two volumes of

Women Writing in India were the earliest to formulate the second position:

We have tried therefore (not always successfully) to strain against the reductive and often stereotypical homogenization involved in the process. We preferred translations that did not domesticate the work either into a pan-Indian or into a 'universalist' mode, but demanded of the reader too a translation of herself into another socio-cultural ethos (p. xxii).

As a result of such articulation of positions there is now a consciousness about the issues involved and a healthy debate has ensued about criteria of judgement in evaluating translation.

The imprints that have high visibility today in this area of fiction translation into English are Macmillan India who have published twenty-four novels in three years, Katha, Seagull Books, Penguin India, Disha Books, Affiliated East–West, Kali for Women, Stree — and institutions like Sahitya Akademi and National Book Trust. Even a research centre like The Indian Institute of Advanced Study in Shimla has of late been publishing translations from Hindi and Urdu. The total number of Indian fiction texts available in English translation is not negligible today, even though these would constitute the tip of the iceberg when compared to what remains untranslated.

It is true that some of the most enduring novels in each of our languages are virtually untranslatable because of their local and specific frames of reference and the play upon variations of language and dialect, which invariably suffer attenuation when translated in English but may not suffer as drastically when translated into another Indian language. One example is Tarashankar Bandopadhyay's *Hansuli Banker Upakatha* (1947) a novel that would figure in my personal list of the ten best novels of the world in the twentieth century, which has never been translated into English, perhaps because the caste/class/tribe interaction in the novel is represented partially through variegated registers of speech. Incidentally, an excellent Hindi translation of this book has been available for some years. Similarly, a Bangla novel called *Aranyer Adhikar* (1979), which for me is the best work of Mahasweta Devi, is still not available in English although some of her short stories are. But this novel was translated into Hindi, Telugu and a few other Indian languages a couple of decades ago. There may be more such examples in languages to which I do not have access.

Indeed, the totality of our fiction texts available in English translation may be an infinitesimal fraction of what actually exists in any of the major languages of India, nor do the texts always represent the best — but quantitatively this entire body can compare favourably with, say, Indian novels originally written in English, which used to be a trickle earlier, but in the last two decades have become a steady stream daily gaining in volume.

Thus we have two numerically comparable sets — Indian novels *written* in English and Indian novels *translated* into English, and the asymmetry in their reception is evident to all. Novelists who choose to write in English, at least the best of them, attract international media attention, their books sell in other countries as well as in India, and get translated into several European languages. Even within India people in the urban areas are far more knowledgeable about the latest novel by an Indian English writer and the amount of advance or royalty he or she is getting than in keeping up with what is available from the Indian languages. There is a vague feeling that such translations are a good idea, and some of them, specially those connected with English Studies, even aspire to do some translations from their mother tongue some day — but if pressed they would admit that they have never read a single novel from another Indian language in English translation. Bookshops display new novels in English prominently, but in order to find the translated ones, one would have to go to the back of the shop and bend in uncomfortable positions to locate a few dusty copies. While writers like Vikram Seth, Amit Chaudhuri, Rohinton Mistry and Arundhati Roy are reviewed and interviewed widely, invited for readings from Seattle to Sydney, not many outside the borders of India, and very few outside the specific language communities within India, have heard of Ismat Chughtai, Gopinath Mohanty, Shivaram Karanth or Shirshendu Mukhopadhyay who write in Urdu, Oriya, Kannada and Bangla, respectively. But language need not be a barrier to accessibility because English translations of at least one novel by each of these writers and in some cases more, are available quite easily for anyone who would care to look for them.

But who should care to look for them and why? Books do not exist in the abstract realm of aesthetic value alone. People read books either because the desire to read a specific text is created through advertisement and discussion in the media, which are then seductively marketed like any other consumer product. Alternatively, they are read if put on reading lists in academic courses. One of the reasons of their relative invisibility may well be that translated novels are brought out mostly by Indian publishing houses that neither have large advertising budgets nor a promotional network to project their books outside the country. The question to ask then is why do multinational publishing concerns — generally based in London or New York — never touch translations from India, when they do, more and more, publish and promote Indian novels written originally in English? The standard reason put forward to explain away this omission — poor quality of translations[4] — does not seem adequate because translation is no longer an entirely amateur activity in India and the entire question of who decides the criteria for good translation throws up issues about the hierarchy of cultures. The natural superiority of an original novel over a translated novel cannot also be sustained as a reason at a time when all the old adages propagating the secondary status of a translated text have been challenged and discarded. 'Translation is the reverse side of the carpet', 'the translator is a traitor', 'poetry is what is lost in translation': such cliches of an earlier era are now anathema to translators and translation theorists the world over who see translation as a creative and interpretative act. In this altered state of consciousness when the earlier metaphors of inequality between the original and the translation (master/slave or male/female, the most offensive being the one that sees faithfulness and beauty being mutually exclusive) are being turned upside down, one has to look for other reasons why multinational publishers do not consider taking up translations from India. Specially when the same publishers have no difficulty in publishing and selling translations from Colombia, Argentina, Poland or Czechoslovakia and securing world-wide media coverage for them.

The category of writers called 'The Third World Cosmopolitans', who are globally visible, who are taught in postcolonial classrooms the world over, and who are hailed in the review pages of western journals as interpreters and authentic voices of the non-western world, hardly ever include a writer from India who does not write in English. This group includes Gabriel Garcia Marquez, Mario Vargas Llosa, Isabel Allende, Derek Walcott, Salman Rushdie, Bharati Mukherjee and a few others. It is interesting that even though this list contains Latin American writers who have been translated into English, the precondition for belonging to this club for an Indian is that s/he must write originally in English. Implicit here is an erasure of the diversity of India.

There is also a pedagogical factor in the dissemination of books: when prescribed in university curricula, novels certainly get a wider currency. Unfortunately, in Indian universities, English departments by and large continue to be orthodox in their course of studies, and even though some might prescribe Homer or Dostoevsky or Ibsen in English translation, inclusion of Rabindranath Tagore's *The Home and the World* (1916) or O. Chandu Menon's *Indulekha* (1889) is strongly resisted on the grounds that a student of English only be given books that are composed in that language. The argument that a translated novel enriches the receiving language is hardly ever considered. The situation is changing a little of late, but only in the more progressive universities.

Less explicable is the absence of translated Indian novels in postcolonial literature courses that are proliferating in the numerous English departments of universities in the USA, Canada, Australia and several places in Europe, partly in response to the increasing multicultural components in their own population, and partly due to an ideological climate that emphasizes the need to open out an Euro-centric academia to the plurality of the world. These universities are far more innovative and the teachers there have greater autonomy in the selection of texts than what the system allows in India. Yet, when these courses include Indian texts, they invariably bring in R.K. Narayan, V.S. Naipaul (who for some reason often qualifies there as an Indian), Salman Rushdie, Anita Desai — and sometimes younger writers in English like Rohinton Mistry or, more recently, Arundhati Roy. The only two writers sometimes to be included who do not write originally in English are U.R.Anantha Murthy (only his novel *Samskara* which was translated into English by A.K. Ramanujan), and Mahasweta Devi (the short stories translated by Gayatri Chakravorty Spivak).[5] In both cases the translators' credentials in the American academy and their appropriate mediation of the texts (through commentary, interpretation and prefatory material) may be as much the reason for such inclusion as the intrinsic quality of the texts themselves, because works by these authors translated by others have not received similar academic attention. For example, Anantha Murthy's second novel *Bharatipura*, also available in English translation, to me a far more complex and nuanced work foregrounding an individual situated at the cusp of history and very different from the fable-like quality that marks *Samskara*, has hardly been critically noticed outside Karnataka. The attraction of *Samskara* to those outside its cultural milieu may well be the timeless, allegorical quality of the protagonist's existentialist dilemma. *Bharatipura* on the other hand, presents an intricate web of predicaments, tangled in caste and class tensions and kinship and ritual patterns peculiar to that region of Karnataka, and a specific moment in time. Although the shifting configuration of a community's public and private value systems are its major focus, the novel cannot be simplified into a predictable bi-polar tradition/modernity dialectic. The stubbornly local and regional novels in the Indian languages, at least the best of them, generally resist such reductive readings, often refusing easy accessibility to those outside the culture. This may be one of the many reasons why some of the best novels from India do not find a ready readership abroad. The novels written originally in English, on the other hand, do not take for granted too many cultural assumptions, because they are addressing a heterogeneous audience. This question of addressivity may well be at the root of the asymmetry mentioned earlier.

Indian writers in English have for a long time been engaged — though not always self-consciously — in the construction of a clearly defined and recognizable India. Raja Rao's definition had a brahmanic frame; R.K. Narayan distilled its essence through a benign small town, middle-class and upper-caste in its composition; some others constructed their India in opposition to what the West was supposed to connote. What appeared homogeneous from a certain discursive perspective easily dissolved into pluralities in Indian-language fiction because the perspective is from within. Because the original target audience of the English novel about India is different from that of the specific audience of the Hindi or Bangla novel, certain shifts in representation become inevitable. Also the socio-economic as well as spatial location of the two sets of writers create differences in their angles of vision. For the urban or diasporic English writer issues of caste, subcaste and tribe, tensions and pressures of a convoluted local variety do not assume the same intricacy and urgency as those directly involved in them.

A comment recently made by Gayatri Chakravorty Spivak can be used here to strengthen the point:

The relationship between the writer of 'vernacular' and Indo-Anglian literature is a site of class–cultural struggle. Indeed the sphere of Indo-Anglian writing and vernacular writing are usually not in serious contact. By class–cultural struggle is meant a struggle in the production of cultural or cultural–political identity. (pp. 126–7)

The novelist in the Indian language seems more involved with the local and the particular, compared to the national project in English which has a greater anxiety to appear 'Indian' because the target readership is diffuse and may include those who have no first-hand experience of India. This anxiety sometimes manifests itself in a pull towards homogenization, an inability to perceive those realities which are situated outside the cognitive limits imposed by English and which cannot be appropriated into the East–West or colonial–indigenous paradigms.

It is not only the earlier writers who felt the need to construct a unitary and recognizable India. In a book published as recently as 1997 (*Love and Longing in Bombay* by Vikram Chandra) the author calls the five sections 'Dharma', 'Bhakti', 'Kama', 'Shakti' and 'Shanti' — disembodied signifiers for India that promise to live up to the unambiguous alterity of the title. *The Mistress of Spices* (1997), the second book by a California-based Indian writer Chitra Banerjee Divakaruni, contains the kind of exotic colours to evoke the country that might have embarrassed an Indian language writer: 'my birthland, land of aquamarine feathers, sunset skies as brilliant as blood'. In this tale of a mysterious eastern woman, the distinctly 'Indian' flavour of the title is intensified by naming the sections 'Turmeric', 'Red Chilli', 'Peppercorn', 'Lotus Root' and ending, for good measure, with a climactic chapter called 'Maya', in case the seasonings have not been sufficiently cooked. For those in India, spices are taken-for-granted ingredients of daily cooking and do not carry any cultural connotation. They assume a symbolic value only when dislodged from their normal context. Since novels in English are read in many regions across the globe, there is perhaps an urgency to announce the specificity of India fairly early in the novel, or in the chapter headings, if not in the title itself.

Certain words, objects and concepts are associated with India in the popular imagination outside the country, which the writer in English may be tempted to deploy as short-cuts to create an ambience. The imperative to essentialize India through evocation of local colour or standard signifiers is naturally less perceptible in the Indian-language novel where intricate tensions of community, religion, caste, language, region and class assume a greater immediacy and the question of Indianness is seldom addressed. In this context Jorge Louis Borges' comments on how 'what is truly native can and often does dispense with local colour' is worth remembering. U.R. Anantha Murthy quotes this passage from Borges as an epigraph to one of his essays:

Gibbon observes that in the Arabian book par excellence, in the Koran, there are no camels; I believe if there were any doubt as to the authenticity of the Koran, this absence of camels would be sufficient to prove it is an Arabian work. It was written by Mohammed, and Mohammed, as an Arab, had no reason to know that camels were specially Arabian; for him they were part of reality, he had no reason to emphasize them ... he knew he could be an Arab without camels. (p. 105)

Does this mean that if the Koran had been written originally in English, the presence of camels might have been unavoidable? One does not know. While all generalizations in literature are hazardous, and one always looks forward to exceptions that would challenge truism, Borges' camels might for the sake of convenience serve as a suitable metaphor for the differential representation I have been trying to describe. In India the constituency of readership is determined by the language of original composition. Even when a Hindi or Bangla text is translated into English, the subtext of assumptions and references do not always get easily transferred to another culture. Thus the fates of the Indian novel in English and the Indian novel in English translation might continue to be dissimilar in the global market. But there is a potentially large domestic market to justify the present surge of translations into English.

Notes

1. For example the poet Vidyapati is claimed both by Bangla and Maithilli, and Meerabai's language has elements of both Rajasthani and Gujarati.

2. 'A Woman Writer's Reply', translated by Gita Krishnankutty in *Cast Me Out If You Will: Stories and Memoirs*, p. 53. The translator in her Introduction to the volume informs us that the Malayalam translation that Lalithambika read was done by B. Kalyani Amma in 1921.

3. My data about this is derived from conversations with Enakshi Chatterjee, the Bangla co-ordinator for the project.

4. Dilip Chitre expressed this view categorically when an earlier version of this paper was presented at the Asiatic Society, Mumbai, in November 1997.

5. The data for these comments on the courses of study is based on my experience of interacting with students and researchers during my teaching assignments and lecture tours in the USA in 1990, 1997 and 1998, in Canada in 1992 and 1997, and in Australia in 1993 and 1996.

References

Anantha Murthy, U.R. 'Search for an Identity: A Viewpoint of a Kannada Writer' in *Identity and Adulthood*, ed. Sudhir Kakar (Delhi, 1979).

Antherjanam, Lalithambika, *Cast Me Out If You Will: Stories and Memoirs*, tr. into English from Malayalam by Gita Krishnankutty (Calcutta: Stree, 1998).

Rushdie, Salman (ed.), *The Vintage Book of Indian Writing* (London: Viking, 1997).

Sapir, Edward, *Cuture, Language and Personality* (Berkeley: University of California Press, 1956).

Tharu, Susie and K. Lalita (eds), *Women Writing in India*, vol. I (New

York: The Feminist Press, 1991, rpt Delhi: Oxford University Press, 1992).

Spivak, Gayatri Chakravorti, 'How to Read a Culturally Different Book' in *Colonial Discourse/post-Colonial Theory*, ed. Peter Hulme and Margaret Iversen (Manchester and New York: University of Manchester Press, 1996).

Index